In with the old,
In with the new.

A no nonsense approach for communicating with real people in the real world.

By Sheila Byfield

First Printing: 2019

ISBN 978-0-244-50195-2
Published by Under The Microscope
byfieldsheila@gmail.com

This book is dedicated to Lucy and Matthew
and also to the memory of Andy Setchell:
an insightful research professional who
was taken from this world far to soon.

Contents

About the author

Sheila Byfield's first job in advertising was with the Evening Standard in 1972. She moved from newspapers to magazines to commercial television joining ATV in 1978.

In 1991 she was recruited to join Ogilvy and Mather to head up UK research and insights. Sheila was instrumental in the creation and maintenance of the future.com study: a large-scale longitudinal panel conducted in a partnership with the University of Leeds. At Ogilvy, she moved quickly to manage research for the European media network and then took on a global role when Ogilvy and J. Walter Thompson merged their media departments to launch Mindshare.

During her time at Mindshare, Sheila managed both industry and proprietary research. She was the architect behind many of the company's successful global research initiatives including 3D, MindSet and MindReader. She sat on the UK Media Research Group Committee, was chair of the European Association of Advertising Agencies' Media Research Committee and is a Visiting Research Fellow of the University of Leeds. She was awarded a Global Lifetime Achievement Award by Mindshare.

Sheila has been a frequent speaker on industry platforms and has a wide range of published work.

Introductory notes

This book was written out of frustration in two areas of life.

First, like many others, I am increasingly irritated by the treatment of the general public from companies and institutions. Customer services are of increasingly poor quality, loyalty appears to have little value, our digital lives are sold to anybody who is prepared to pay and human interaction has been sacrificed in favour of artificial intelligence alternatives.

Secondly, I am extremely disappointed by the direction that the advertising and media businesses have taken in recent years. Increased efficiency is a sound objective and there is no doubt that technologies save both time and money. However, there should have been a better balance between the quantitative (data) and the qualitative (creative) sides of the business.

This wouldn't matter an iota if it wasn't having an effect on the effectiveness of the end product when it reaches a potential customer. Trust and respect in advertising are at an all time low. Ad avoidance has escalated to an all time high. This book is a plea to address these issues from the perspective of real people and to address them before the damage is irretrievable.

It has taken an age to complete. I swear that a steamy sex novel would have been far easier for me to write and, without a doubt, a lot more enjoyable for you to read.

It wasn't only procrastination that slowed progress. In the process of writing I was being told, constantly, that everything is changing - and changing fast. I began to doubt my own opinions and was nervous of looking like I was totally out of touch with the real world.

In the midst of this episode of self-doubt, I came across a media magazine from the 1990's and realised that many of the issues that were facing us then are the same as those with which we struggle now. There is a new toy box, a different vocabulary and a digitised generation trying to make sense of it all but the really big issues have withstood the test of time. All we seem to have done is to make everything a lot more complicated.

Eventually I realised that there isn't anything wrong in repetition if you believe the subject is still important, relevant and worth re-enforcing. So I kept on writing.

This isn't a 'how to' book. It is a 'why don't you use some basic common sense?' book.

I must make it clear that, unless otherwise stated, the views expressed are all mine. They do not reflect any organisation, institution, company, individual or any of the people who have kindly contributed to the content.

It isn't 50 Shades but I hope that you will like it.

"It died with the arrival of digital advertising"

Is it too late to save

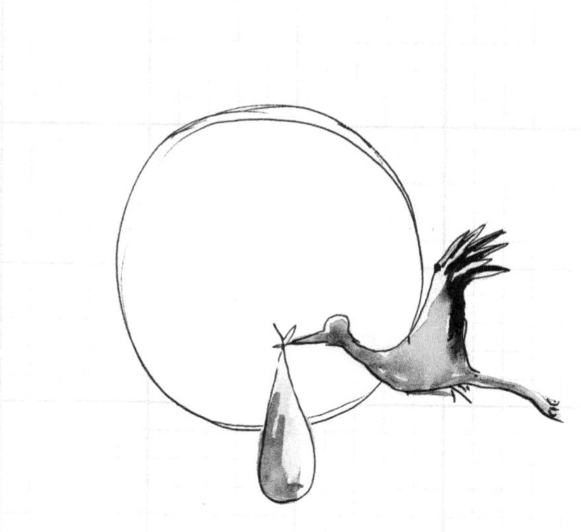

the baby?

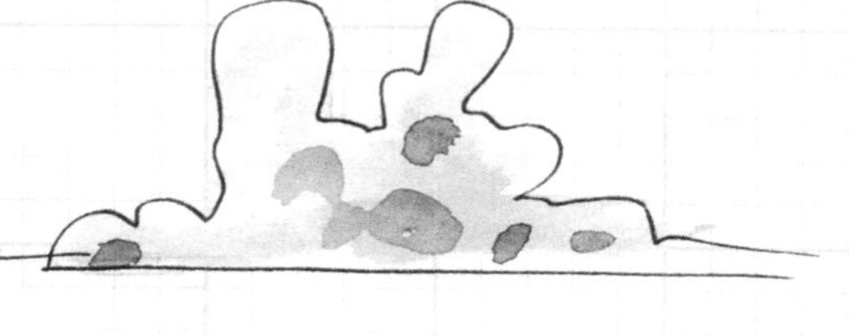

"Change is inevitable, progress is not"

Max McKeown

Is it too late to save the baby?

I visited the offices of a media agency recently and felt rather sad. It was very quiet. Lots of young people were staring at screens. There was no buzz or excitement in the air. There was very little to indicate that this was part of an exciting business and even less to suggest any connection with advertising.

Jeff Goodby, the Co-Chairman of Goodby, Silverstein & Partners, a San Francisco advertising agency, expressed similar sentiments in The Wall Street Journal following his visit to an ad industry award ceremony in Cannes a couple of years back.

He said, 'Cannes used to be a showcase for some of the most famous ideas in the world. This year it felt more like a convention of industrial roofing specialists discussing the latest in fibreglass insulation technology.'

Hey Jeff - let's not be too hard on the roofing specialists.

How has this happened? How have we turned a vibrant business bursting with excitement, passion, creativity and fun into one that is focused on data, process and algorithms?

Agencies were once centres for critical thinking and logical reasoning. Now it appears that data have replaced insight and the quest for originality and learning has been largely dismissed. It used to be Mad Men. Now it seems more like Mad-Ness.

It is very sad that the media have become so commoditised and that the emphasis is on easier, faster, automated solutions rather than on what different communication routes can add to awareness, brand values, customer perceptions and sales. Once we focussed on effectiveness and used systems as an aid to speed up and simplify the process. Now it appears that the systems direct the show.

Maybe it is not surprising that trust in agencies has declined and there are questions over how effectively media budgets are allocated.

The promise was very different. It was all going to be so exciting. We were going to leave the world of interrupting people and move into joyous engagement with them. We would go from monologue to dialogue, stop talking at and start talking with, the end of shouting and the start of listening. This was all good news as, apparently, people weren't paying attention to our mass marketing messages anyway.

It gets even better. Brands would be able to hold conversations with their target groups who would then become brand fans, create their own content and spread the word. I'm coming clean here. There are brands that I like. There are brands that I like a lot. But I don't have conversations with them on-line or anywhere else. I reserve conversations for people. I don't think that I am alone in this and it is not an age thing.

A Financial Times article quoted a senior marketer from Diageo who said, "After 10 to 15 years of f***ing around with digital we've realised that people don't want to 'engage' with brands, because they don't care about them".

> **"Modern marketing is operating under the delusion that consumers want to interact with brands, and have relationships with brands, and have experiences and engage with them, and co-create with them. Sorry amigo. Not in this lifetime."**
>
> Bob Hoffman
> The Ad Contrarian
> 'Marketers are from Mars. Consumers are from New Jersey'.

Anyway, digital things arrived by which time the media business had hyped itself up into quite a frenzy. But when it all died down, if indeed it did, things were not quite as had been promised.

The interruption model that was set to die, if anything, became more prevalent in on-line media. Digital advertising response rates are shockingly low, agencies have been accused of fraudulent practices, ad exposures are often robotic rather than human, personal data are misused and abused and still no-one seems to have cracked how to measure all of this stuff accurately.

It was quite a lot of hype but, undeterred, companies large and small jumped on the bandwagon and poured millions of dollars into the digital pot. There was little or no evidence on how, or even if, these media worked - but that didn't matter. No one wanted to be left behind. The emperor had a new set of clothes and was parading them for all not to see.

There is no suggestion here that digital media channels are not exciting, influential or effective. They have had a fundamental and irreversible influence on our lives and they can be powerful advertising vehicles when used well.

Increased choice, the power of the individual and an instantaneous, 'anything-anytime-anywhere', always on culture available to everyone have created behaviours that are unrecognisable compared with even ten years ago.

All of this has altered the shape of the commercial communications business forever and has posed huge challenges for planning, trading and measurement along the way.

Of course we want to exploit the potential commercial opportunities offered by this ever-evolving media world. But to improve advertising effectiveness, not waste clients' ad budgets and regain trust, we need to apply intelligent thinking (dare I say common sense?) to address key issues such as if, when and how people will respond to commercial messages in this increasingly erratic landscape.

There is a significant body of empirical evidence on how advertising and the media work. Should we dismiss this knowledge as irrelevant because there are some new kids on the block? Wouldn't it be better to understand what is still relevant, what we should re-enforce, what we should do differently and where the emphasis should lie?

On-line communications deserve the same rigorous approach as any other medium. It's fine to allow algorithms to place the final message but without human intelligence to drive intelligent insights, strategic thinking and to oversee tactical implementation, programmatic can become problematic and brands may end up in ineffective, and potentially detrimental, places.

As Rory Sutherland, Vice Chairman of Ogilvy puts it, 'an algorithm would suggest advertising your latest booze product at Alcoholic Anonymous meetings'.

> **"Marketing in social media is no different than any other form of marketing such as e-mail, online, billboards, direct mail or TV. All those avenues have carefully planned strategies and measurements for success. Why shouldn't you use the same approach for social media?"**
>
> Liana "Li" Evans
> Social Media Marketing

This book is not a plea for a return to the, so called, 'good old days'. Its aim is simply to provide some common sense in a hyped-up, confused and complex world. It is written from a belief that communications will be more effective if we combine sound learning from the past with the exciting opportunities made possible by the present.

More importantly, it is a plea for us to stop annoying people and start listening to them when they tell us they want (or rather don't want) from the media channels they use. Audiences have been generous with their time and trust so surely we should reward them with respect and then we may stand a better chance of persuading them to pay attention to our expertly crafted messages.

'In With The Old, In With The New' explores the core reasons why people use media channels and how they respond to advertising. It goes all the way from planning which channels to use through to the final interaction between the brand and its customer to complete the communications circle. Advertising, along with all other aspects of marketing, is a total waste of time and money if you disappoint your customer in the final stages.

> **“If dogs don’t like your dog food, the packaging doesn’t matter”**
>
> Stephen Denny

It also suggests ways of thinking about media behaviour that are relevant (hopefully) when communicating with a socially connected and always-on audience.

Along the way, leading industry experts have been kind enough to share their views and there are both proprietary and industry data to illustrate the points being made.

My mantras throughout are simplicity, common sense and, above all, absolutely no jargon.

We mustn’t throw the baby out with the bath water. Let’s rescue the baby and go back to selling stuff

Back to

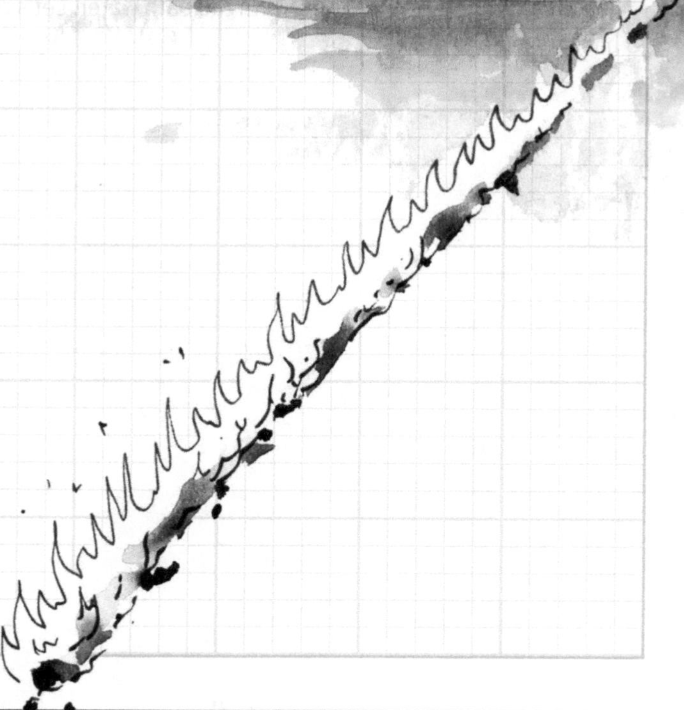

the future

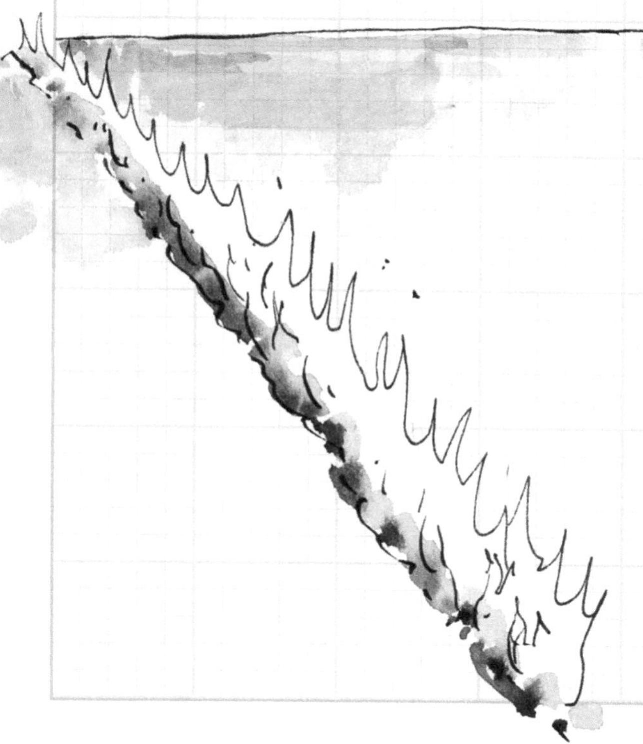

“

There are three mistakes that people make when trying to imagine the future. The first is to believe that it will not be constrained by what has gone before, that it will be entirely different. The second is to believe that it will be exactly the same, that nothing ever really changes. The third, and the worst, is not to think about it all’

”

Horsman, Matthew and Marshall, Andrew (1994):
After The Nation-State: Citizens, Tribalism and the New World Order.
Published by London. Harper Collins.

Back to the future

In 1994 the BBC aired a programme called 'The Future of Advertising' as part of their 'Late Show' series. The 'future' was set in the year 2000 and it looked extremely bleak from an ad agency perspective. There were scenes of an office that was deserted and covered in cobwebs.

In contrast, life in the home looked very bright indeed. Happy, smiley families were relaxing in their 'living rooms of the future'. Each had a huge TV screen that covered a whole wall. Every 'viewer' was interacting with the television screen.

Media experts appeared throughout the programme and predicted the implications of this new exciting, interactive, television world on advertising as we knew it. Basically they all thought that it was completely screwed ....

"It could be the death of broadcast advertising as we know it ..... We can't be sure that ad supported TV will have a future"

Edwin Artzt
(Then) Chairman. Proctor & Gamble

"What we are going to see is a total switch in traditional advertising practices ..... the end of traditional advertising where advertisers send out messages".

Michael Schrage
(Then) Media Columnist. Adweek

"...... a trend we are already seeing of the slow death of the spot advertisement which is the world's most inefficient way of reaching customers .... I don't think that there is any doubt that people will use interactive adverts more than they use conventional ones .... Commercial revenues will fall ...... Commercials could become a thing of the past"

Andrew Curry
(Then) Manager of Interactive TV. Videotron

"The viewer becoming the editor rather than the broadcaster is a real prospect indeed .... viewers having the power to direct their own commercial breaks"

Rob Norman
(Then) Media Director. CIA

This group was not alone in its views. At around the same time George Gilder published 'Life After Television' and confidently told us that computer and fibre optic technologies spelled certain death to television and telephony.

"In coming years, the very words "telephone" and "television" will ring just as quaintly as the words "horseless carriage", "icebox", "talking telegraph" or "picture radio" ring today."

"Revenues from telephones and televisions are currently at an all time peak. But the industries organized around these two machines will not survive the century."

George Gilder
Life After Television: The Coming Transformation of Media and American Life
(Published 1994)

The speculation in the Late Show programme focused on the year 2000. There was universal agreement that TV advertising was finished. As I write this 25 years later, television is not only still with us but, in the main, appears to be doing rather well.

People are still watching in significant numbers and for significant amounts of time. Given that the medium is supposed to have died by now, the corpse isn't doing too badly at all. It's still moving.

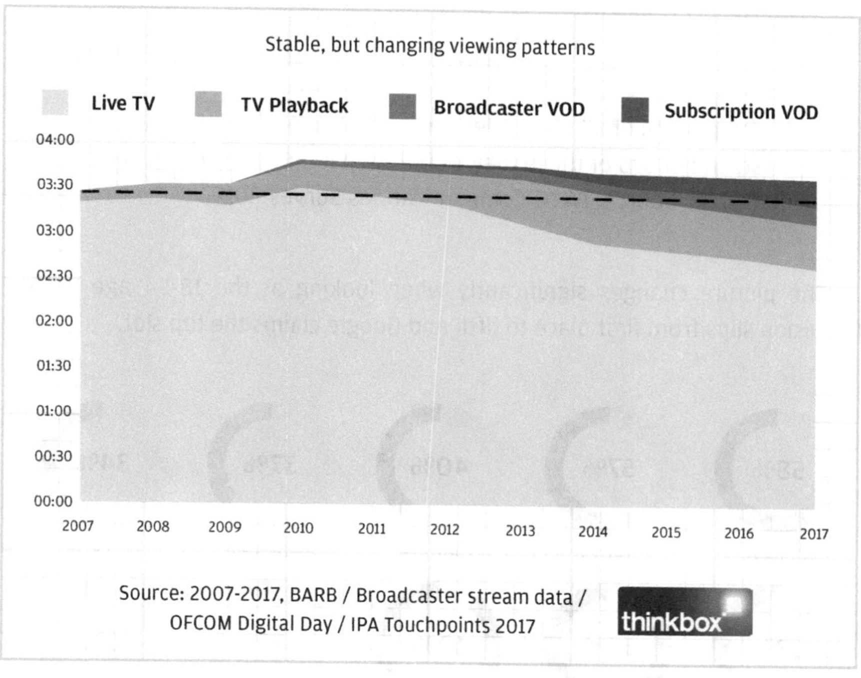

In February 2019 Populus conducted a survey for this book on a nationally representative sample of 1,078 UK adults. Respondents were asked which media they would choose if only allowed to keep three. TV performs best for appearing in the top three:

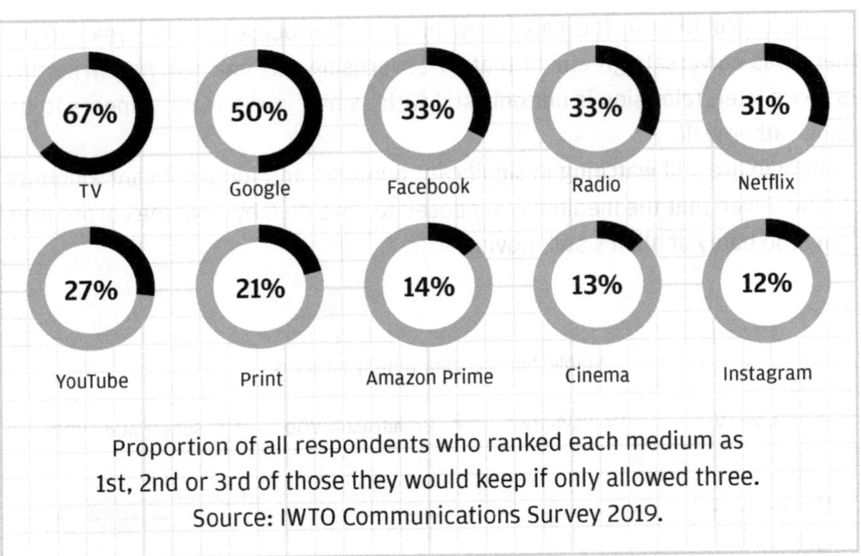

Proportion of all respondents who ranked each medium as 1st, 2nd or 3rd of those they would keep if only allowed three. Source: IWTO Communications Survey 2019.

The picture changes significantly when looking at the 18-34 age group. Television slips from first place to fifth and Google claims the top slot.

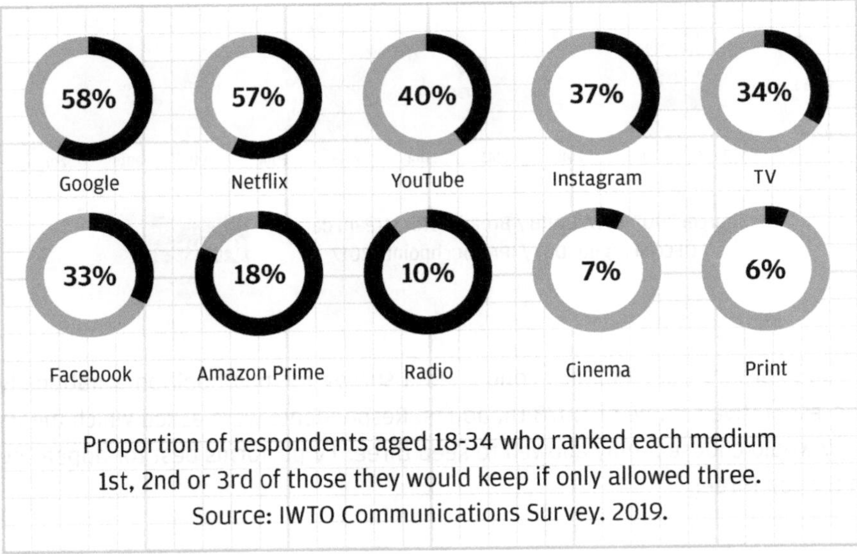

Proportion of respondents aged 18-34 who ranked each medium 1st, 2nd or 3rd of those they would keep if only allowed three. Source: IWTO Communications Survey. 2019.

Interestingly, Facebook has the same percentage for all adults and the younger group. Certainly its demographic profile is older now. Is this what Mark Zuckerberg wanted for his cool brand?

TV is still a very important medium in people's lives but clearly not quite as much with younger cohorts.

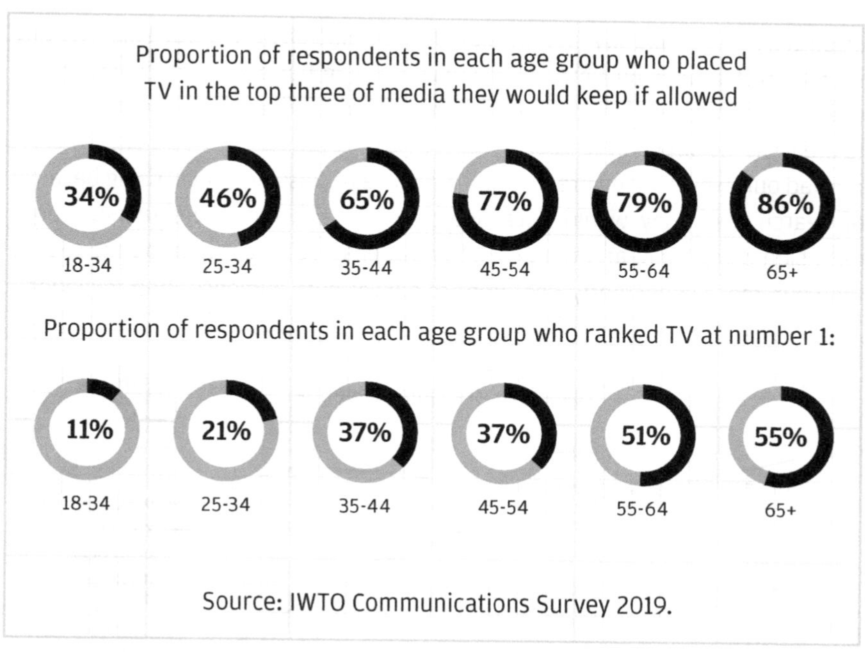

Source: IWTO Communications Survey 2019.

Could this be yet another example where the direction of change was correct but the speed was grossly over-estimated? When the experts on 'The Late Show' talked about the end of commercial TV advertising by the year 2000 maybe they should have speculated about 2030. But that would have been a forty-year trend. What would have been the fun in that? This is the ad business for goodness sake. Everything must change quickly. We need to hype it up.

Predictions like these are typical of an industry responding to hype and are not unusual. There were dire warnings that cinema was doomed because of video but the movie business went on to enjoy one of its most successful eras despite the competition. Books were set to disappear because of e-versions and, while it is true that audible books are doing well, dead tree sales are also increasing. Vinyl was going to disappear completely first because of CDs and later because of streaming but is having a wonderful revival - surprisingly driven by the young.

Of course there are examples where the new does replace the old but more often they sit compatibly side-by-side. I do on-line shopping but enjoy visiting shops. I watch films on Netflix and Amazon Prime but adore the cinema. I use e-books when convenient but love the tactile and flexible qualities of paper (not to mention the smell).

Had our experts been predicting the decline of classified advertising because of Search then they would have been spot on but they were talking about television advertising and that, as we know, has not only withstood the test of time but, more importantly, continues to deliver both audiences and revenues.

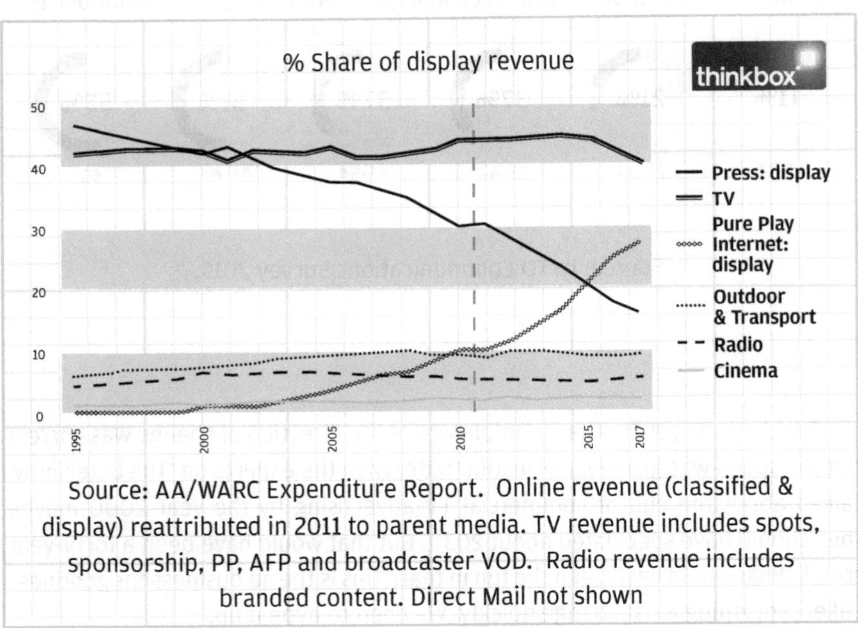

Source: AA/WARC Expenditure Report. Online revenue (classified & display) reattributed in 2011 to parent media. TV revenue includes spots, sponsorship, PP, AFP and broadcaster VOD. Radio revenue includes branded content. Direct Mail not shown

Interestingly the tech giants are seeing the benefits of these boring old, out of date media too. The eight major tech brands nowadays place a large and growing investment in 'traditional' media.

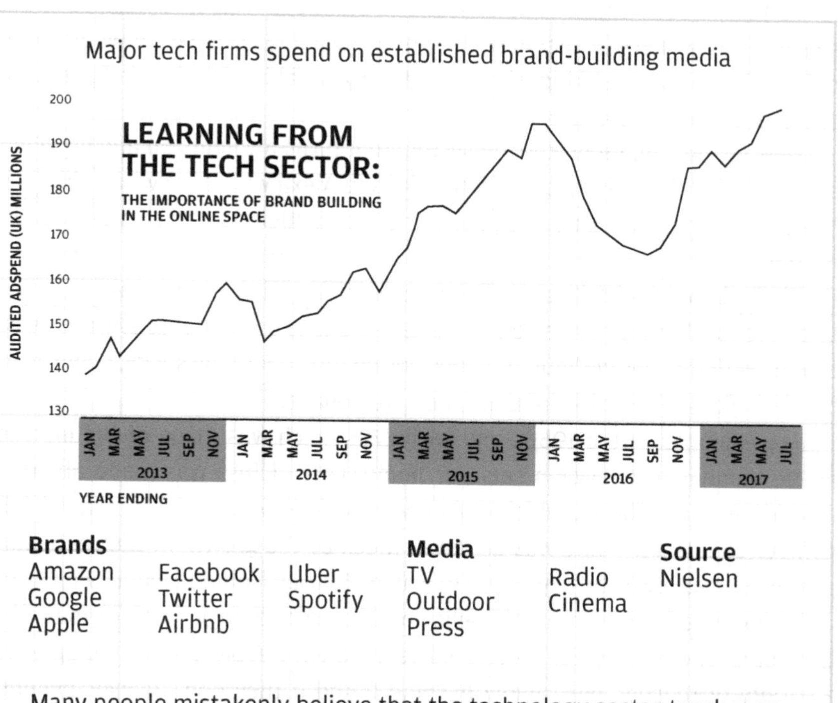

Many people mistakenly believe that the technology sector teaches us that brand building is unimportant in the digital era. In fact the tech sector teaches us completely the reverse. The eight major tech brands in the UK evidence a considerable and growing level of investment in established, 'traditional' brand building media by the sector. Do they know something that many online businesses don't?

Les Binet. Adam&Eve DDB. Peter Field. Peter Field Consulting
Effectiveness in Context. A Manual for Brand Building.
Published by the IPA

To be fair to the soothsayers, it is difficult to imagine the future even when presented with it.

I remember seeing a device called 'Butler in a Box' in the early 90s. This clever little gadget sat in in the living room and, upon hearing your voice, could turn on the TV, turn lights on and off and so on. It even had a name. I remember shaking my head in disbelief at such a stupid idea and asking what would be the point in having such a thing when I am totally capable of flicking a light switch and turning on my television.

Now I have a home protection system that turns my lights on and off when I am away and I frequently issue instructions to Alexa who (surely that should be 'which') I address by name and adore. The little butler was simply way ahead of his time.

There is no doubt that prediction is a tricky science yet, when trying to understand what the future holds, it is dangerous to assume that everything will change with the new without first considering the underlying social, cultural and psychological drivers that influence how we behave.

For example, in the 1960s and early '70s much was made of the increase in the number of television sets per home. Lots of fuss was made about TV increasing in popularity, which indeed was true. However, the increase in the number of sets per home was driven as much by the growth in central heating penetration as it was by any desire to watch TV away from the main living room.

Deep seated motivations and behavioural drivers change rarely despite what is on offer and, if they do, they do so very slowly. People use technologies for a variety of reasons but rapidly become bored if they don't deliver benefits. We don't want technology for the sake of it. We want products that will make our lives easier, more convenient or more enjoyable. Benefits must override features. Novelties are often short lived.

> **Human nature hasn't changed for a million years. It won't even change in the next million years. Only the superficial things have changed. It is fashionable to talk about the changing man. A communicator must be concerned with the unchanging man, with his obsessive desire to survive, to be admired, to succeed, to love, to take care of his own.**

Bill Bernbach
Doyle Dane Bernbach

It's a sobering thought that the first experiments into interactive TV were conducted in the 1970s and yet, almost fifty years later, it still hasn't truly captured public interest. People claim to like these new toys when in a research laboratory but fail to adopt them in the real world especially when asked to pay. People find it very difficult to say what they really want.

> **If I'd listened to my customers, I would have given them a faster horse.**

Henry Ford

For some strange reason, the predictions that heralded the death of advertising on the one hand presumed that people would suddenly find it exciting on the other. With the exception of very early commercial TV when ads were a novelty, people have been trying to avoid them. Why would they start interacting now? They sure aren't going to start clicking on things that they wish would go away.

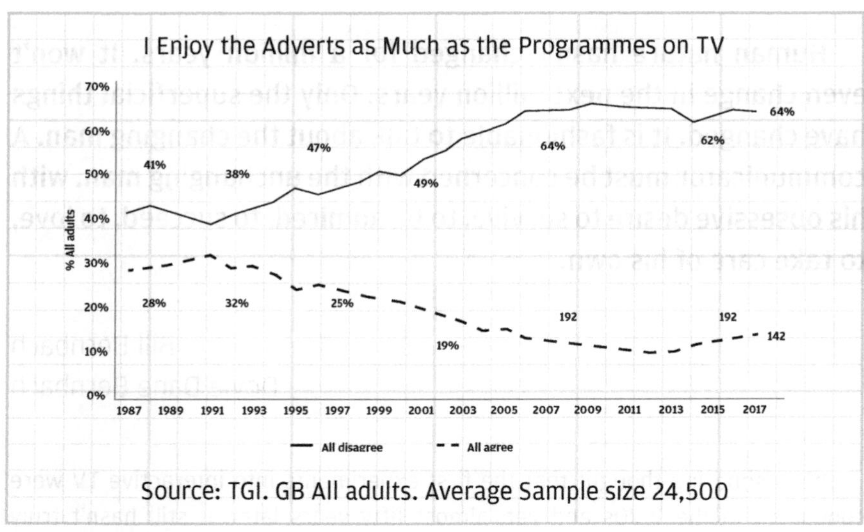

Source: TGI. GB All adults. Average Sample size 24,500

At the same time long-term trend analysis from The Advertising Association Think Tank, Credos, shows that favourability towards advertising has also been in long term decline:

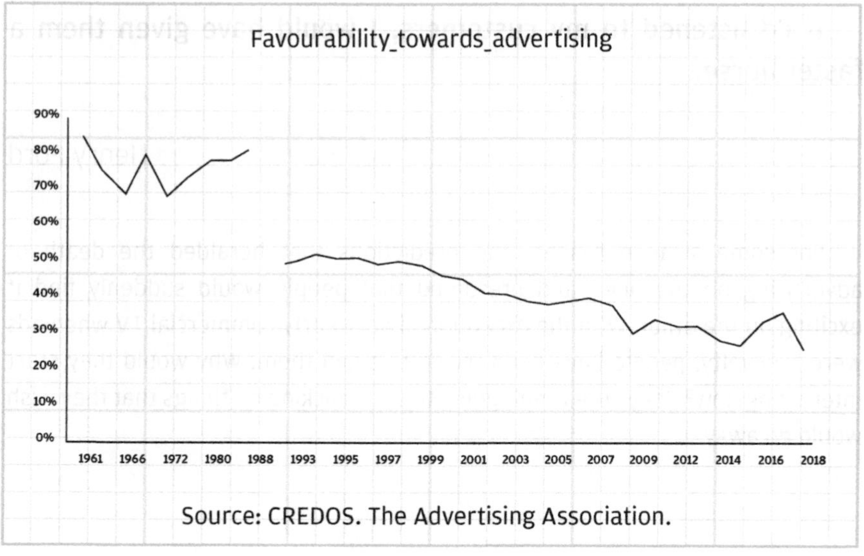

Source: CREDOS. The Advertising Association.

Remember the red button on the TV screen that provided additional information about advertised brands or programmes? Mindshare asked respondents to use it several times a day as part of their Screens research. Only 2% of use was in response to advertising. The remaining 98% was to seek additional programme information. It is doubtful whether people would have used it at all had they not been instructed to do so as part of the study.

Against this real world that stares us in the face, the media business exacerbates the hype with an insatiable need to always be saying something new. Anyone who worked in media a decade or so ago and even hinted that things may not turn out quite as the digital fortune tellers would have us believe was greeted by looks of sympathy, disbelief and horror.

For years the marketing communities were under pressure from their CFOs who questioned the cost - though not always the value - of advertising. More recently, those same finance guys encouraged an increased emphasis on digital media. They had heard that millions of people were using them and lots of exposures were going for 'free'. Nobody had proof that they worked but that didn't matter. Size of audience was everything. It was a dream come true. They couldn't jump on the bandwagon quickly enough - best not to be left behind.

Agencies responded in the usual way - quickly. They changed their structures and brought in data scientists and digital media specialists. Good old-fashioned practitioners were moved to one side to make room for the digarati.

Out with the old. In with the new.

Quite rightly, everyone had to be brought up to speed with the New New Thing although strangely, digital teams didn't seem to spend time understanding the effectiveness of other media.

I think this was a huge oversight. Had more time been devoted to understanding the new alongside the established (and especially the balance between them), instead of assuming a replacement model - maybe budgets would have been better allocated and companies wouldn't have suffered from either a lack of effectiveness or, in some cases, a decline in sales following a switch into social media.

Initially, the results looked impressive in the much-quoted Pepsi example when the TV Superbowl campaign was cancelled in favour of the 'Pepsi Refresh Project'. There were 3.5 million Facebook Likes and the campaign was quoted as an overwhelming success as it doubled the number of Facebook brand fans. WOW!! The only problem was that Pepsi suffered a 5% loss in market share and moved from 2nd to 3rd place in the cola category. Oops.

The Pepsi story was widely reported and attracted much comment from industry pundits who pointed out that although the internet has changed how the game is played, it has not changed the fundamental rule that mass marketing works.

Personally, I am not convinced that all of the blame can be laid at the door of social media. I don't know what it was but feel that something else must have been going on at the same time. Having said that, the fact remains that digital media are great at some types of commercial communication but not all. More of that later but there does seem to be a massive disconnect between what the agency fraternity thinks is going on and what is happening in the real world.

I think there is great value in academic institutions and commercial enterprise working together to make sense of issues such as media and technology adoption trends. Of course the academic and commercial worlds operate at different speeds with different priorities. However, academic involvement can help prevent agencies from jumping on the bandwagon for the sake of a good story. From an academic perspective, commercial involvement can help with funding, speedier analyses and increased commercial uses of data.

Academia is a good starting place to start when seeking truth. I am a long time admirer of Patrick (Paddy) Barwise, Emeritus Professor of Management and Marketing at The London Business School. Paddy has an impressive history of publishing academic theory on marketing, leadership, media, technology and advertising. His conclusions are always pragmatic and grounded in sound reality. He has authored and co-authored many books including 'Simply Better', 'The 12 Powers of a Marketing Leader', 'Television and its Audience' and 'Beyond the Familiar' amongst others.

In 1998, Paddy along with Kathy Hammond also from The London Business School, published a book of media predictions for the year 2010. I asked him whether their view of the future was accurate.

An expert view

Professor Patrick Barwise

Emiritus Professor of Management and Marketing. London Business School.

Q. It is now twenty-one years since 'Predictions'* was published, how accurate were you and what surprised you?

A. I will start with where I think we were reasonably accurate. At the time, most of the speculation on the future of media was focused on the expected convergence in the devices we use and how they would affect our behaviour. Much of the conversation centred on whether the TV would also be a computer or whether the computer would also be a television and then which we would use to fulfil all of our entertainment, information-seeking and on-line transactional needs.

Predictions were rife that the television, as we knew it, was dead and would change dramatically from passive linear to active non-linear viewing. The digerati told us that we would be able to watch sports programmes from different camera angles, click on a T shirt worn buy Jennifer Aniston and buy it while watching Friends, click on international news items and instantly access information about foreign countries and so on. We were even told that people soon (i.e. by the year 2000) wouldn't be using the word 'television' any more.

We didn't see it like that. First, we didn't see that the nature of television viewing would change all that radically. We didn't see it then and I am not seeing it now. Secondly, we didn't see convergence of devices or behaviour in the home. (It's different outside the home: with mobile there really is a benefit in carrying a single multipurpose device like the iPhone).

If you look at long-term trends in viewing you will see that, actually, there has been very little change. In the first quarter of 1992 the average US adult aged 18+ in a TV household watched 34.9 hours per week of TV/video – slightly less than five hours per day. 95% of this was to live TV. The other 5% used a VCR either time-shifted or watching rented video content. **

Since then, terrestrial, cable and satellite TV have all gone digital, offering hundreds of channels increasingly viewed in high definition on large flat screens or smaller sets around the home. DVR's, DVDs and Blu-ray disks have replaced the VCR and the internet has brought many new ways of watching online, anywhere and anytime.

25 years on in quarter 1, 2017 total viewing among US adults 18+ had increased by 17.5% to an average of 41 hours per week - almost six hours per day.*** And despite all the speculation about the death of traditional television, 84% of this viewing was still to so-called, 'linear' broadcast programmes on a TV set either live (74%) or time-shifted using a DVR (10%).

The exception to this general pattern of increased viewing is amongst younger adults such as 'millennials' whose media usage is changing faster. In Q1 1992, US adults aged 18-34 watched an average of 30.2 hours per week (4.3 hours per day). The equivalent figure in Q1 2017 was 29.1 hours per week - a small 3.6% reduction. But viewing of live TV within this group was down 43% from 28.1 to 16.1 hours per week. The increase in other viewing, mainly online, made up for most of the reduction in traditional viewing.

But while millennials' viewing differs markedly from that of older adults, and is changing faster, they still watch TV / video for over four hours per day - almost as much as the same age range 25 years earlier. What's more, the majority of their viewing is still offline.

Back in 1998, we thought that the idea of behavioural convergence was nonsense when talking of devices inside the home. Why would we want the same device for watching movies and for ordering groceries? There is room in the home for both. We mostly use fixed devices that are optimised for their application. And I don't have to tell you that we are not dictating the camera angle when we watch football nor are we buying Jennifer's clothes.

Overall, I think we were pretty accurate in our vision of the future shape of media behaviour.

Q. What about the areas where you were less accurate?

A. Most people were overestimating the speed of change especially with television viewing and convergence. We took a more pragmatic view on all that which turned out to be right. But there were other areas where I think we underestimated the speed and the direction of change. (Remember that people thought that it would take only ten years for a computer to beat the world chess champion when in reality it took forty).

We - and many others - thought that networks in the home would run through cable. We underestimated the speed of wireless technologies and how quickly they would replace cable in the home.

On the other hand, we thought natural language processing would develop faster than it did so we overestimated how quickly voice interface control would arrive. The market is now roughly where we thought it would be in 2010. To be fair most of the techies were even more overoptimistic.

Another trend that took longer than we expected was how long it took for print 'classified' advertising to be replaced by online search and online classifieds. We underestimated the inertia in this market. While we were directionally right, our ten-year estimate should have been twenty years.

At the time our book was seen by the digerati as excessively British, negative and stick-in-the-mud. We were accused of 'just not getting it'. In reality, while acknowledging that we underestimated the speed of wireless and smartphone technologies, we were broadly right on consumer behaviour (particularly television viewing) and also on the shape of the media business.

Q. What do you think are the most positive and negative developments in the communications business in the past five to ten years?

A. The positives and the negatives are the same – digital. The good news is that we can do all sorts of things that we couldn't do before. The bad news is that we can do all sorts of things that we couldn't do before.

On the positive side, digital has brought lots of new tools, most field research has gone online, there are many digital applications in the insights space and promotional activities can be conducted much faster.

In the 'narrow' marketing space where budget allocation sits, the internet is brilliant at communications that are initiated by the customer. This means that advertisers have to make sure that their web sites are top quality and that they optimise Search and CRM activities. Twitter is also a great way at keeping in touch with customers especially when there is a need for time-sensitive information e.g. the use by Virgin Atlantic to keep passengers informed during the Icelandic dust cloud. ****

It's different for 'Push' advertising. The communications have to fit into social norms - it's rude to interrupt - and display advertising has to look good and engage people. This may be possible with online Video on Demand but as it evolves towards television it becomes television. We have a medium called television and viewers don't care if it's delivered through broadcast or online. What does matter is the impact of different screen sizes and their effects upon viewer reactions.

Short-term videos are a bit different but we don't yet understand the way people de-code marketing messages on Youtube and the like. We don't know how much viewing would decline if viewers were 'forced' to watch fifteen seconds of commercial material before their requested content appeared. Clearly, the measurement of online video exposure needs to be addressed. It is nowhere near good enough.

All of these issues were ignored by the digirati who thought it was going to be one beautiful, converged, digital porridge. Marketers, on the other hand, have to understand which of their marketing needs are being met and which customer needs are being met. They need to be able to identify changing behavioural patterns because they can give valuable clues on media channel resource allocation.

* 'Predictions'. MEDIA. Published in 1998 by Pheonix.

** 'Why Do People Watch So Much Television and Video? A Review of the Evidence'. Patrick Barwise, Steven Bellman and Virginia Beal. Journal of Advertising Research. July 2016.

*** Source: Nielsen Media Research national people-meter panel of 12,600

households.

**** 'The One Thing You Must Get Right When Building a Brand' by Patrick Barwise and Sean Meehan. Harvard Business Review. December 2010.

Mind

the gap

Embrace reality
even if it burns you

Pierre Berge

Mind the gap.

In one of his newsletters, Bob Hoffman, The Ad Contrarian, highlighted some research conducted by Research Now. 250 people from agencies and the marketing professions were asked to estimate video viewing behaviour on television versus SmartPhone. They were shockingly inaccurate. The 'professionals' estimated that 25% of video viewing was on a television set and 18% on the 'phone. In the real world the percentages were 82% and 2% respectively.

Thinkbox, the television marketing body in the UK, have conducted similar analyses with very similar results.

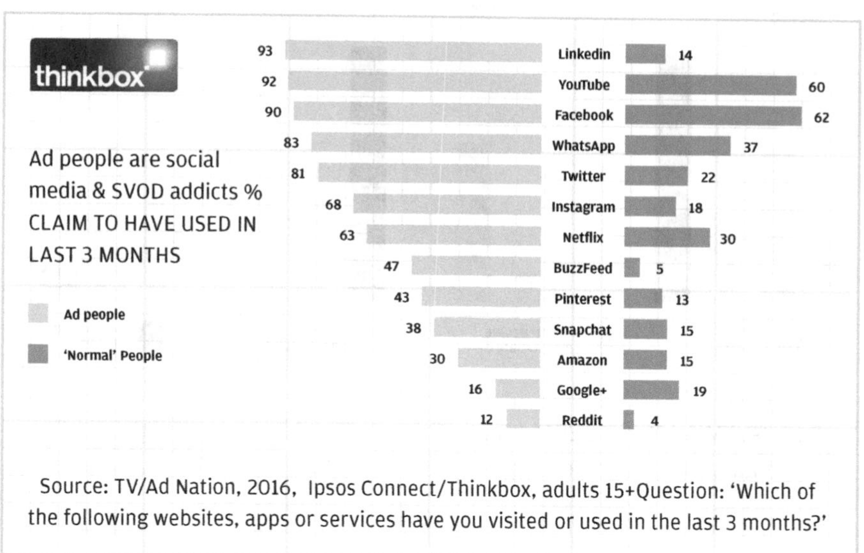

Source: TV/Ad Nation, 2016, Ipsos Connect/Thinkbox, adults 15+Question: 'Which of the following websites, apps or services have you visited or used in the last 3 months?'

The media behaviour of those in ad land bears no resemblance to people in the wider world. Almost without exception, their use of social and digital media channels far outweighs that of the population as a whole.

The ad folk were completely inaccurate when asked to estimate the TV viewing behaviour of the general public. They significantly underestimated both the amount of time spent watching TV each day (2 hours 41 minutes versus 3 hours 54 minutes) and the proportion of viewing that is live (49% versus 87%). At the other end of the scale, viewing to Netflix and Amazon Prime was vastly overestimated (1 hour 24 minutes versus 11 minutes). Similarly, the estimated proportion of viewing that is spent multi-screening was estimated at 50% by ad people but was only 19% according to BARB data. (Note: all figures are from the time of the survey).

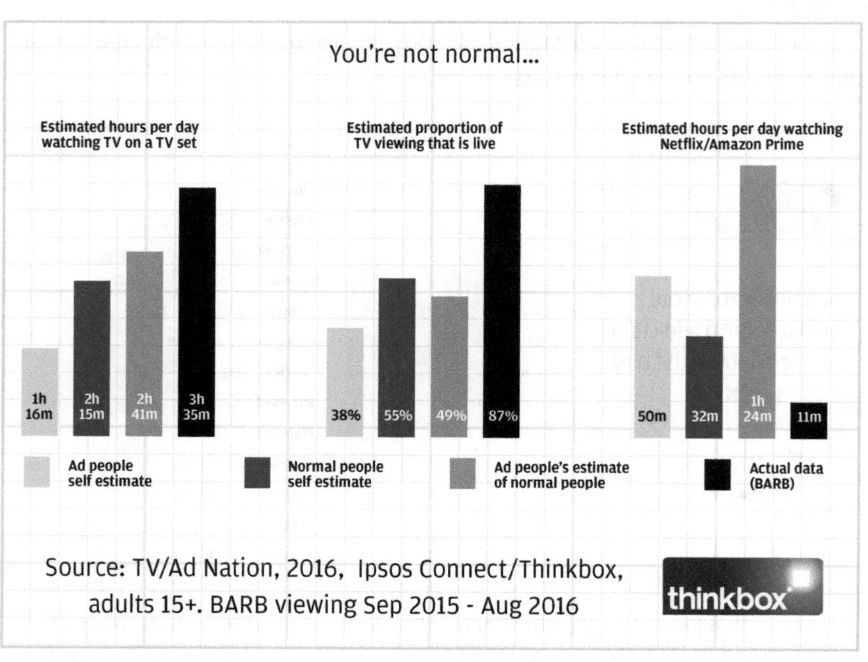

Are these findings really so surprising? According to the IPA census, a staggering 84% of media employees are under the age of 40. Agency people also tend to live in capital cities where life is very different from elsewhere. They are hardly representative of a wider society.

Trinity Mirror Solutions studied 2,000 UK adults and 150 media agency representatives and found that the agency folk have a very different value system to the mass market responsible for the vast majority of brand expenditure. They were way off course when asked to estimate the values and concerns of the population at large - overestimating power and hedonism and underestimating self-direction, universalism and benevolence.

People in ad land are more focussed on power and achievement with a stronger sense of personal control over life than the average person. Of course younger people have always been different from oldies – to be different is one of the golden rules for being young. And it wouldn't matter a jot if they weren't responsible for planning and executing communications to reach mass audiences while assuming that most people think and behave exactly like themselves.

The yawning knowledge gap between perception and reality was further highlighted by 'Re-Evaluating Media' - a report from Radiocentre and Ebiquity. Unlike many other investigations funded by media marketing bodies, Radiocentre left Ebiquity totally to their own devices in the design and execution of the research. There was no interference and respondents did not know who had commissioned the research. It is an honest piece of work without a hidden agenda. Ten media were examined: magazines, newspapers, radio, television, cinema, social, online display, online video, out-of-home and direct mail.

Interviews were conducted with sixty-eight marketers with ad budgets of at least £2 million along with 48 executives from both media and creative agencies.

The results were combined with an exhaustive range of other research sources ranging from The IPA Touchpoints study through to over fifty different research sources and many more published reports. Professor Mark Ritson, brand consultant and columnist, gave it a thumbs up for methodology and if it's good enough for him ....

It is well worth downloading the full report to examine the twelve dimensions studied. They range from Return on Investment and Targeting to Emotional Response and Saliency. In most cases, however, there was a disconnect both in what the marketing and advertising communities believe are the most effective media and what the real data tell us. While TV topped the tables in both perception and reality, the strengths of social and digital media were overstated by the sample.

In the Ebiquity study, all twelve attributes were combined to produce the ultimate league table as follows:

The real world		The world of marketers and agencies	
1	TV	1	TV
2	Radio	2	Online video
3	Newspapers	3	Social media
4	Magazines	4	Out of home
5	Out of home	5	Cinema
6	Direct Mail	6	Radio
7	Social Media	7	Newspapers
8	Cinema	7	Direct Mail
9	Online Video	9	Online display
10	Online display	10	Magazines

Source: Re-Evaluating Media. Radiocentre and Ebiquity. 2018

Time after time we are presented with evidence of the unrepresentativeness of our profession – an indication that we, as the advertising community, need to take heed of the evidence. If I was a brand custodian I would not allow anyone to work on my business without having total immersion with my target audience.

Interestingly for the sponsors of the report, targeting was the only area where radio triumphed out of the channels measured but it came bottom in the perceptions of effectiveness from the 'experts'.

	Targeting
The real world	**The world of marketers and agencies**
1 Radio	1 Direct mail
2 Social media (paid)	2 Social media (paid)
3 TV	3 TV
4 Online displa	3 Online video
4 Cinema	5 Online display
6 Direct mail	6 Cinema
6 Out of home	7 Out of home
6 Online video	7 Magazines
9 Newspapers	9 Radio
10 Magazines	9 Newspapers

Source: Re-Evaluating Media. Radiocentre and Ebiquity. 2018

Gary Vaynerchuk is a prime example of this 'out of touch with the real world' phenomenon. For anyone not familiar with Vaynerchuk, he is widely recognised as the charismatic, social media guru of the day. He has millions of followers across every digital platform and is the author of 'Jab, Jab, Jab, Right Hook' amongst other books.

He has run or owned a variety of businesses ranging from wine to media and seems to have the magic touch in that all have grown exponentially. He is a phenomenal success and clearly someone to whom we should pay close attention. Audiences listen agog whenever he speaks.

But here's the thing. Vaynerchuk purports a number of theories (or facts as he sees them) that are based purely on his own opinions and behaviour. They include:

- Apart from The Superbowl, the only channels worth using for advertising are Facebook and Instagram.
- No-one watches television any longer – apart from The Superbowl of course.
- The TV networks are about to go out of business.

- If anyone is watching television, the minute an ad break appears, everyone – yes that's EVERYONE – reaches for a Smartphone. (Ads in Superbowl are presumably exempt from this behaviour)

Really?

Gary preaches this mantra to young audiences of digital converts like himself and also to leading Fortune 500 companies. Good for him. He is making a lot of money. But if clients are looking for effective communications advice surely the behaviours of everyday people should be taken into consideration.

It is worrying that people with unrealistic views are advising clients on media allocation. Gary focuses on a target group that he believes reflects the behaviour of the general population but, not only does their behaviour differ, they do not account for the majority of spend in many leading categories.

I asked TGI for some age profiles for a range of product categories and found, with few exceptions, the volume of use to be higher amongst older groups even for some sectors that one would think would be younger.

	16-44 years	Over 45 years
After shave	50.4%	49.4%
Perfume	45.5%	54.5%
Instant coffee	35.6%	64.3%
Fresh coffee	38.1%	61.8%
Car ownership	39.3%	60.8%
Take holidays abroad	44.5%	55.5%
Lager	46.5%	53.5%
Heavy wine drinking	29.9%	53.1%
Play video games	61.9%	38.2%

Source TGI

In one of his regular pieces for Marketing Week, Professor Mark Ritson wrote a piece disputing each of Vaynerchuk's claims using empirical evidence, sound learning, experience and acute observation from the real commercial world. I recommend his article. (Search: Ritson Vaynerchuk). Ritson invited a response from GV but, strangely, it has been quiet. Maybe I missed it.

You know what though? Gary may have a case if he is going to be advising clients in 10-15 years. We have already acknowledged that the speed of behavioural change may have been overestimated in the short-term but it is possible that its impact may be phenomenal in the long. Certainly attitudes amongst the young vary significantly from the population at large in the world of on-line media. When the young children of today are in an older cohort their digital behaviour may be more extreme than that of their equivalent age group now.

	All	**18-34**
Most of the advertising I see is relevant to me	19%	38%
Social media do a good job to make sure that advertising I see is relevant to me	22%	53%
I would like more regulation on what appears in social media	71%	55%

% = Net agree

Source: IWTO Communications Survey 2019.

At the same time, there are some aspects of the online world where the opinions of the young are not so very different to those of the general population:

	All	18-34
I would be prepared to pay a small amount of money to social media companies to stop them using my personal data	13%	15%
Overall my life is better because of the internet	64%	70%
I am annoyed when ads appear unexpectedly when I am online	75%	66%
I am concerned over the way that some people use social media	77%	71%

% = Net agree
Source: IWTO Communications Survey 2019.

Perhaps Gary Vaynerchuk is another 'Butler in the Box' and just way ahead of his time.

Andrew Tenzer who heads up Group Insight at Reach Plc (formerly known as Trinity Mirror), feels that the advertising and media businesses need to confront this current disconnect with a matter of urgency. He is concerned that this unconscious bias, if not addressed, will lead to a situation where many brands become invisible through using the wrong vehicles to talk with their potential customers (I think it is happening already).

It should be proven media performance, and not emotionally driven bias, that dictates where budgets are spent. Many in the media businesses are out of touch with reality. We are not normal.

In 2018 a Marketing Week article featured a quote from Gerhard Louw, Head of International Media at Deutsche Telekom. Becoming somewhat frustrated with the behaviour of digital media companies he said, "If you guys don't sort it out, guess what? We're going back to TV, all out".

While understanding his frustrations, surely this isn't the right attitude. Of course the tech giants should be held accountable for their actions and address problems but allocation of ad budgets should be based on what works, delivers against business objectives and positively influences customer perceptions and behaviour. If TV works then use TV. If digital channels work best then use them but please don't move valuable funds around without evidence on what is effective and what the impact will be.

To put it very simply from an advertising perspective, digital media are just more channels that people use. Yes they use them in huge numbers. Yes they spend lots of time with them. Yes they are exciting because they provide a whole plethora of instantaneous, sophisticated products and services that previously were either unavailable or very hard to access. We would find it very difficult to do without them nowadays.

But to persuade people to buy our brands through digital screens, we need to spend time understanding how these new avenues work, what people want and will accept from them - just as media researchers have been doing for decades with print, radio, cinema, outdoor and television - the old with the new.

It is time to take a step back, dismiss the hype and re-evaluate how people use and respond to different media. We may then use them in the context of how they **actually** perform as opposed to how we **think** they perform.

> “**It is better to be roughly right than precisely wrong**”
>
> John Maynard Keynes.

But just before we do that, let's have another break.

Mindshare was formed in 1997 when Ogilvy and J. Walter Thompson merged their media departments. The business has changed significantly over its 22-year history. I asked Nick Emery, Global CEO, to reflect on his observations of the changes that have occurred over the period since Mindshare launched (and by the way, he always looks this grumpy!).

An expert view

Nick Emery

Global CEO.
Mindshare Worldwide

Life in a media agency – then and now.

We used to say that media isn't rocket science. Well it is now.

When we created Mindshare there were broadly three types of career in media – planner, buyer and researcher; I'm not sure we even called it insights back then though Sheila will correct me, she usually does.

Now you can be anything – data scientist, IP owner, platform generator or retail guru – everything now begins and ends in media. Our clients' reputations go up and down on the barometer of social media; e-commerce is the central plank that drives growth and our clients expect a seamless integrated engine that moves from audiences to content to sales. This all makes media and the understanding and capture of audiences the key cog in the overall marketing relationship.

We grew up as experts in aggregated mass audiences, creating big ideas for iconic brands. We still have to do that but the central question for every CEO and CMO now is how we balance and integrate both brand and demand – the mass reach and the individual addressable message. Our job now is to create bespoke engines that move seamlessly from audience identification to iterative content creation and from production to sales. Media touches, evaluates and influences every aspect of every customer journey. All humankind can be mapped, understood and become part of a conversation.

This all requires new skills and a much broader talent base now than ever before. Media has to be a home to many talents. We are essentially now a talent agency. We create virtual joint ventures with our clients based on their needs and ambitions. We are trusted with their first party data and we create teams that work seamlessly with theirs, often in their offices.

This is a huge change and makes media what it always had the potential to be – the most exciting job in the world. Media is a job that spans Amazon to 21st Century Fox, WeChat to Facebook and Netflix to the Super Bowl.

Media was once the domain of the lads, a boys culture with lunches of raw meat and chianti and a language steeped in masculine and military jargon. We are by no means perfect but we have come a long way. We are now a place that celebrates the individual, the punk and the maverick. We place our highest value on creating new things and having fun doing it, not on shouting loudest for the cheapest price and on being a home for anyone and everyone.

A small bunch of us were once the misfits, now we are all misfits who love change and love how media can change the world.

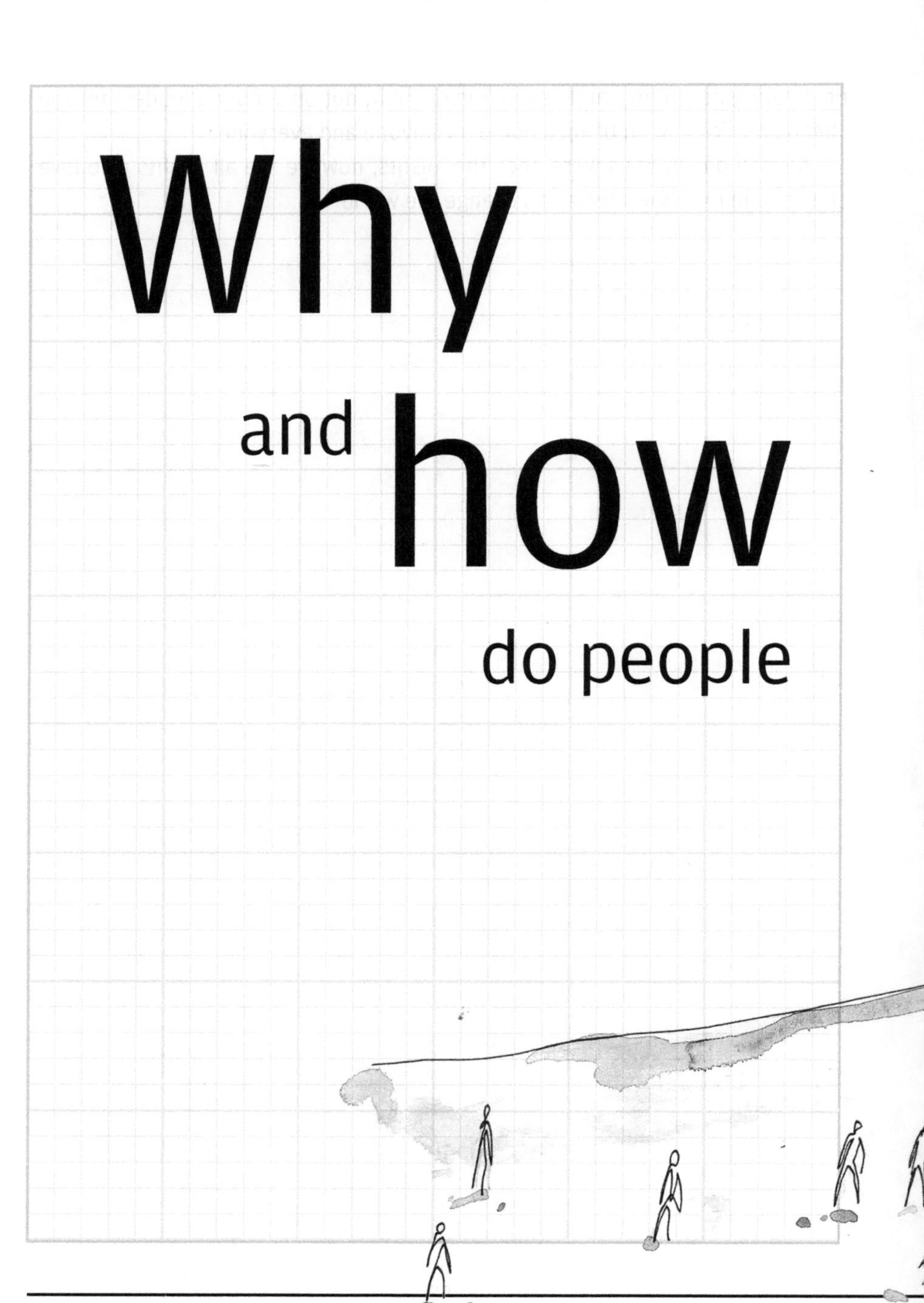
Why
and how
do people

use
media?

Whoever controls the media, controls the mind.

Jim Morrison
American singer-songwriter

1. Why do people use media?

Irrespective of whether you are a digital junky or a couch potato, there are five core reasons why you use media channels. The Henley Centre for Forecasting identified them as:

Entertainment
Information
Communication
Transactions
Self-Expression

The ways we fulfil each has been changing since time immemorial:

- Entertainment went from music hall to cinema to radio to television and recently to any screen at all.
- Information has transformed from encyclopaedia to Wikipedia.
- Once the carrier pigeon had died, communications were the sole property of mail services but moved then to the 'phone, e-mail and now social media.
- Transactions were once conducted through street vendors followed by small local shops then supermarkets and department stores. Now a thriving and growing business has been built through e-commerce.
- Self-expression has probably seen the most radical change. Once upon a time we could only express our opinions through the written word or speech. It was a difficult life. We had to ask everyone individually if they liked our cats and tell each of our friends personally what we had for lunch. Nowadays we can share endless pet videos and photographs of our meals. What joy.

Importantly, though, the five basic drivers of media behaviour have not changed and are unlikely to do so.

Digital media deliver across all five functions. We can watch video, play a game, search for information, hold a conversation, send an e-mail, shop and share photographs of our food all through the same screen and almost simultaneously.

> **“Like air and drinking water, being digital will be noticed only by its absence, not its presence”**
>
> Nicholas Negroponte
> (Then) Chairman of MIT Media Lab
> Wired magazine 1998

None of this means that advertising placed in digital media will be more effective. It just means that we have many more places where we can showcase it. Every medium works for some types of advertising but not all. Digital media are no different. We must be careful not to confuse ubiquity with effectiveness.

2. How do people use media?

Irrespective of demographics, lifestyle, interests, occupation or whichever discriminator you care to use to identify your target customers, it would be rare to find all of them using media in the same way.

Age is still a powerful discriminator. Older groups may still be wedded to print. Younger generations rarely touch a newspaper or magazine and instead turn to a screen for news.

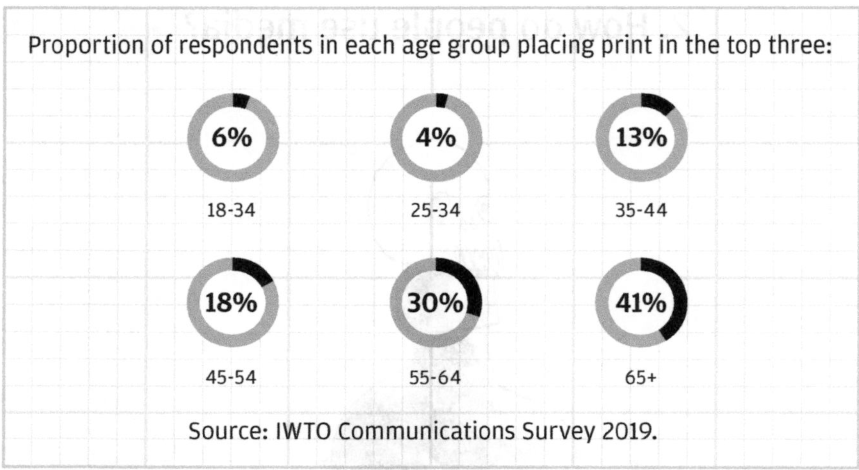

From a marketing perspective however, it isn't any longer a case of 'traditional' versus 'online' marketing. In smart companies and agencies, they are completely integrated.

Expansive versus Reductive behaviour.

Our media behaviour sits on a spectrum driven largely by the task in hand and the time available.

On the one hand sometimes we are in a relaxed frame of mind - let's call it 'Expansive'. This is when we are most at ease and, importantly, more open to ideas.

The most expansive environment is probably the cinema with its dark, quiet, undisturbed atmosphere and big visual stimulation. Our most expansive moments are when enjoying entertainment channels e.g. when watching television or browsing online for pleasure. These relaxed environments are not all equal but are the most appropriate for brand advertising, sumptuous imagery, making emotional connections and so on.

At the other end of the spectrum we have a more time-pressured, concentrated, hurried frame of mind. We will call this 'Reductive'. At these times we are more stressed and our minds are focussed on the task in hand. Any commercial communications must be totally relevant otherwise they will be intrusive and irritating.

One of the most influential trends to affect us in all walks of life is growing time pressure. In most parts of the developed world people claim that they don't have enough time.

% agree 'Nowadays I feel as if I don't have enough time to do everything I want to do' by age group.

Total	52%
18-24	62%
25-34	66%
35-44	64%
45-54	58%
55-64	36%
65+	33%

Source: IWTO Communications Survey 2019.

Life has become busier and more complex and there is simply more competition for our time and attention. As a result, time can become a more valuable commodity than money. Of course this varies significantly by demographic group and it is the time poor/money rich that are most affected but nevertheless, it is a general, important and growing trend.

In his book 'Busy Bodies', Lee Burns, the American economist and urban planner, argues that time and its management are the most important drivers of social change. He believes that almost all technological and social innovations can be attributed to a desire to maximise the use of time. People do this either by increasing the satisfaction gained from any given unit of time, or by reducing the amount of time spent to achieve the required level of satisfaction.

This trend raises issues over how people manage the choices available to them. We tend to think of people choosing from hundreds of television channels, radio stations, coffees or breakfast cereals when, in reality, they have a smaller repertoire from which they choose. The trick of course is to earn a place on the consideration list.

It is true that people want greater variety but increasingly they need help to navigate so that time is spent efficiently.

Trusted brands win in these situations. Their ads can help too. They provide reminders and familiar signposts in a sea of choice when time is limited.

It is interesting to consider where different media sit in our hectic schedules. Are they 'slow' and associated with reflection or 'fast' providing convenience and speed? This is important because people will respond differently to advertising depending on the time pressure context.

If I go to GoogleFace to find a plumber because water is flooding my home, the only ad I want to see is for a local, highly recommended plumber who is good value and can be with me quickly. I am time pressured and anxious so please do not try to sell perfume to me (even if I have previously visited your perfume site!). But at another time, when I am browsing luxury hotels, then I may pay attention to a pertinent ad that you serve me. It is the same medium, I am the same person but my task is different and therefore my response to your message will change based on my time pressure and frame of mind.

Think about your own media behaviour for a moment. You are far more relaxed and 'expansive' when watching TV in the evening than when reading your trade press in the office.

Morning drive time radio is used to provide time-sensitive information such as news, weather, traffic and so on. That's probably not an ideal time to time to try and sell holidays. At the other end of the day, however, that same car radio provides a far more relaxing experience. The working day is over and your mind is open to consider different options. The Caribbean cruise sounds lovely. Once again, it is the same medium, you are the same person but this time, unlike my search for a plumber, you are relaxed and that will affect how you respond to messages.

People use on-line media in the same way - from one end of the Expansive / Reductive spectrum to the other - but whether advertising is welcome is dependent on the task in hand. The key is to target messages based on why people are there and not just because they happen to be present. The level of time pressure will dictate how they respond.

This needs human intervention. Algorithms are improving all the time but, while they can tell you that someone is likely to be present, they have to guess the state of mind, level of involvement and the reason for the visit.

I wish the holiday and airline industries would understand this. Obviously, algorithms have told them that I am a news junkie in the morning and that I like travelling so they keep hitting me on news sites with holiday ads. Please go away. I am in a reductive frame of mind and you are turning me off your brands through irritation. On principle I will not respond because I want to prove to you that your advertising isn't working. I am involved in the medium but am in a reductive frame of mind and so not responsive.

A host of studies have been conducted into the importance of audience involvement and media context. One example, the Quality of Viewing Study conducted by The Media Partnership* in the 1990s, concluded that people who were involved in a TV programme were up to 30% more likely to remember the advertising they had seen.

In another Ogilvy study, groups of respondents were shown a photograph of a woman wearing an ordinary dress and asked to estimate the cost as if it had appeared in a specific publication. So one group was shown the ad in a tabloid newspaper, the second in a quality newspaper, then a mid-market magazine and finally an up-market glossy magazine.

The perceived price of the dress ranged from £15 in The Sun to over £100 in

---

*The Media Partnership (TMP) was a research and knowledge- sharing partnership between the media disciplines of Omnicom (BMP and BBDO) and WPP (J. Walter Thompson and Ogilvy and Mather) advertising agencies.

Vogue. The study took place in the 1980s, hence the low price estimates, but it demonstrated clearly that the media carry brand values, just like any other type of brand, and advertising effects can be amplified through positive association. Context is a powerful influence on how people will perceive and respond to ad messages.

This may be a potential problem for digital media marketing. They may be less effective because many people perceive them to be free. TV on the other hand is deemed to be expensive. Everyone has a feeling that it is expensive to place a thirty second ad in Love Island or, even more extreme, a spot in the Superbowl.

The sub-conscious understanding is that the advertiser is making a serious investment, must be serious and therefore the product is more likely to be good. Anything that signals investment in a relationship tends to generate greater trust. Rory Sutherland sites the engagement ring as a prime example. It must be 'reassuringly expensive' in order to signal the seriousness of the relationship. The same is true in advertising. The perceived quality of the advertised product is in direct proportion to the quality of the medium and the associated investment in it - when a lot has been invested the takeout is that it must be good, more reliable and trustworthy. At least it is less likely to be bad.

'It's too cheap to be of good quality' is a very good statement to use in brand research.

Anyone responsible for placing advertising would be wise to ask not only where the ad will appear but also the context. Not to do so may risk an irrelevant response, or no response at all. Context was taken into account in the past when planners were working with a pen, paper and a slide rule. I exaggerate to make a point but the question remains over whether algorithms have sufficient 'understanding' of context to ensure maximum success? My instinct is not.

Another time when we are, potentially, in an expansive frame of mind is when reading for pleasure but, even then, the media context may have a significant effect on how well we digest and remember content.

It is sad to see the decline in paper magazine sales. In my view, the luxury end of the monthly magazine market is one of the most expansive media environments. I wonder if all of that beautiful brand imagery is received in the same way when it appears on a hard screen and away from its glossy, tactile environment. I am just not sure that these ads will work in the same way if not on paper. They just won't 'feel' the same.

Anne Mangen of Norway's Stavanger University has conducted a large body of research into the effects of reading on paper versus a screen. In one study where respondents were asked to read a story either on paper or on an i-pad, she found that paper readers had higher scores than e-readers on measures to do with empathy, immersion and narrative coherence. The researchers suggested that the tactile attributes of Kindle do not provide the same support for mental reconstruction as print.

In another study, Mangen gave 72 Norwegian 10th graders text to read either in print, in PDF format or on a computer screen. Reading was followed by comprehension tests. She found that 'students who read texts in print scored significantly better in comprehension tests than students who read them digitally'.

Mangen is now studying the impact of e-reading on children as screens are used with increasing frequency in both education and home settings. While this is far more important to society than advertising effectiveness, we should look at these findings more closely if they suggest that the impact and comprehension of on-screen messages are different to alternatives. It begs the question as to whether advertising will also be less understood and therefore less impactful. Our objective must be to find environments when the audience is in an Expansive frame of mind and the media context compliments the mind-set. The print media industry may do well to study Mangen's work at a time when both readership and advertising revenues are in decline.

It is important to recognise that both people and the media can be Expansive or Reductive at different times and on different occasions. The trick is to understand motivations (why are they there?), mind-set (are they relaxed or time pressured?) and then apply the message appropriate to the circumstances.

By the way, this doesn't mean that we shouldn't advertise in Reductive / time pressured environments. Rather it suggests that any communication should be short, sharp, to the point and relevant. You wouldn't use an outdoor poster space for a detailed recipe. The length of exposure would make it totally inappropriate. Similarly when you are searching quickly on-line, your time-pressured mindset means that you probably won't take kindly to interruptive, irrelevant, brand building, display advertising.

Good media planners have understood this for decades and have successfully directed appropriate messages to marry the frame of mind with the media environment in which the ad sits. The same rules should apply to the on-line world. Surely it isn't beyond the realms of today's sophisticated algorithms to categorise digital media in this way so we can marry context more closely with brand attributes and objectives.

We should be able to improve the advertising effectiveness of digital channels if we can apply the learning from other media. There is no reason why the rules should change because the delivery mechanism is different. The mind-set, importance of time pressure and the nature of the task in hand apply to all media.

Boardie Willie
An example of 1890s advertising

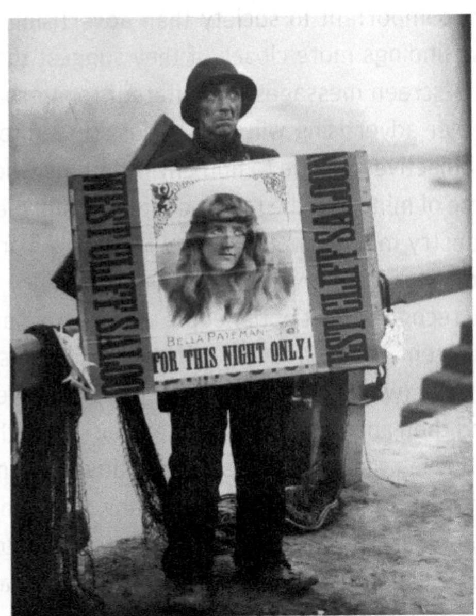

Reproduced by permission of Whitby Museum WHITM:FMSP84

An expert view

Alison Ashworth

Chief Strategy Officer.
OMD.

Q. What are the most positive changes you have seen in your business over the past 5-10 years?

A. Great strategy once used empathy to solve business problems. Creativity then turned the strategy into ideas and the media broadcast the ideas out to real people. Now technology means that the media can put ideas into peoples' hands for them to explore more deeply and to interact. It has made brands and ideas more exposed to scrutiny. Data have given us the ability to see what people are experiencing in real time.

Q. And the most negative?

A. In contrast, the biggest change has been the move away from empathetic to systematic thinking and the subsequent shift to favour the linear, logical and efficient. To see data as insight. To see people as targets. To see efficiency as effectiveness. Our business has been navel gazing with its obsession with digital versus analogue. Real people don't live in channels. The good news is that we are slowly recognising this and calling for a rebalance: a pivot back to understanding real people. The route to this is diversity, not just in our people but in diversity of thought. It's the only way for us to empathise with people.

Q. Is advertising more or less effective than it was?

A. I have to say less because of all the evidence: lack of trust in advertising, the rise of ad-blockers, the debate about the morality of ad-tech, all point to people not liking advertising anymore. That's got to be less effective. Les Binet and Peter Field have proven the damage that the move to short-termism is doing. Long term we must get back to effectiveness over efficiency.

Advertising has taken advantage of digital technology, now we are bombarding people with messages, experiences, faux relationships. We have hit the law of diminishing returns. This is a great opportunity for those focused on making only ideas that matter and for rewarding people for the gift of their time.

Q. What part have digital channels played?

A. They've opened worlds of possibility to engage, connect, reward. Again, Binet & Field have proven that using digital channels enhances the effectiveness of good ideas. But we've abused those opportunities somewhat by not having empathy with how people are using digital technology and platforms. We have deeply intimate relationships with our technology but advertising in digital channels is still largely disrespectful of that.

Q. There has been a lot of comment about the change in focus in agencies between planning and data-driven solutions. Do you think that planning is still receiving the focus and credit that it deserves?

A. Great planning still gets focus and credit - if it is great. Our skills are even more in demand and we are brilliantly placed to extract meaning from data, to simplify complexity, to solve problems with creativity. However, data-driven, systematic thinking has reduced diversity of thought. Analysts and planners need to collaborate more so that planning works in the real world. We'll get the credit if we unlock more value.

Q. What steps should agencies take to bring about a closer relationship between planning and digital functions?

A. Seeing 'digital' specialism has been very damaging to our business. We do what we do to effect real people who live in the digital world. Digital thinking should be incubated not specialised. It needs to permeate the whole agency as it has permeated the real world. It cannot be a separate thing. There are new skills required to understand digital complexity and analyse all of these data in the same way as when TV came along. We need to bring in these new skills but ultimately we have to incubate digital in the same way as real people have. There is no such thing as a digital person.

Q. What advice do you wish you had been given when starting your career?

A. Working in advertising demands bravery and resilience. I'm not sure I'd have gone into it had I known how much of that I would need to find. Our business lives in a bubble dominated by strong egos and lacking diversity of thought. As a strategist, my role has always been to empathise with real people: to respect, simplify, clarify, create.

Q. What advice would you give to someone entering the business now?

A. My advice then and now is to remember the real people but, above all, make it fun. Despite the emotional roller-coaster, advertising is still an amazing way to make a living.

Q. Finally, what keeps you awake at night?

A. Problems I am wrestling with, words I am trying to find and colleagues doing my head in.

How

do people

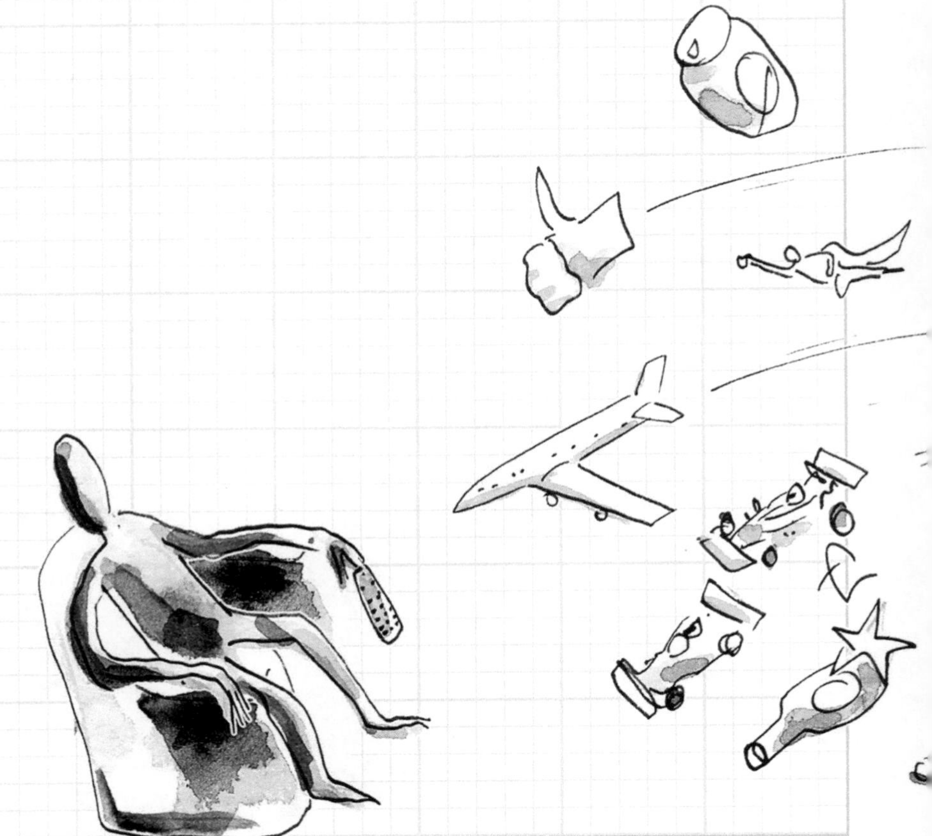

respond to advertising?

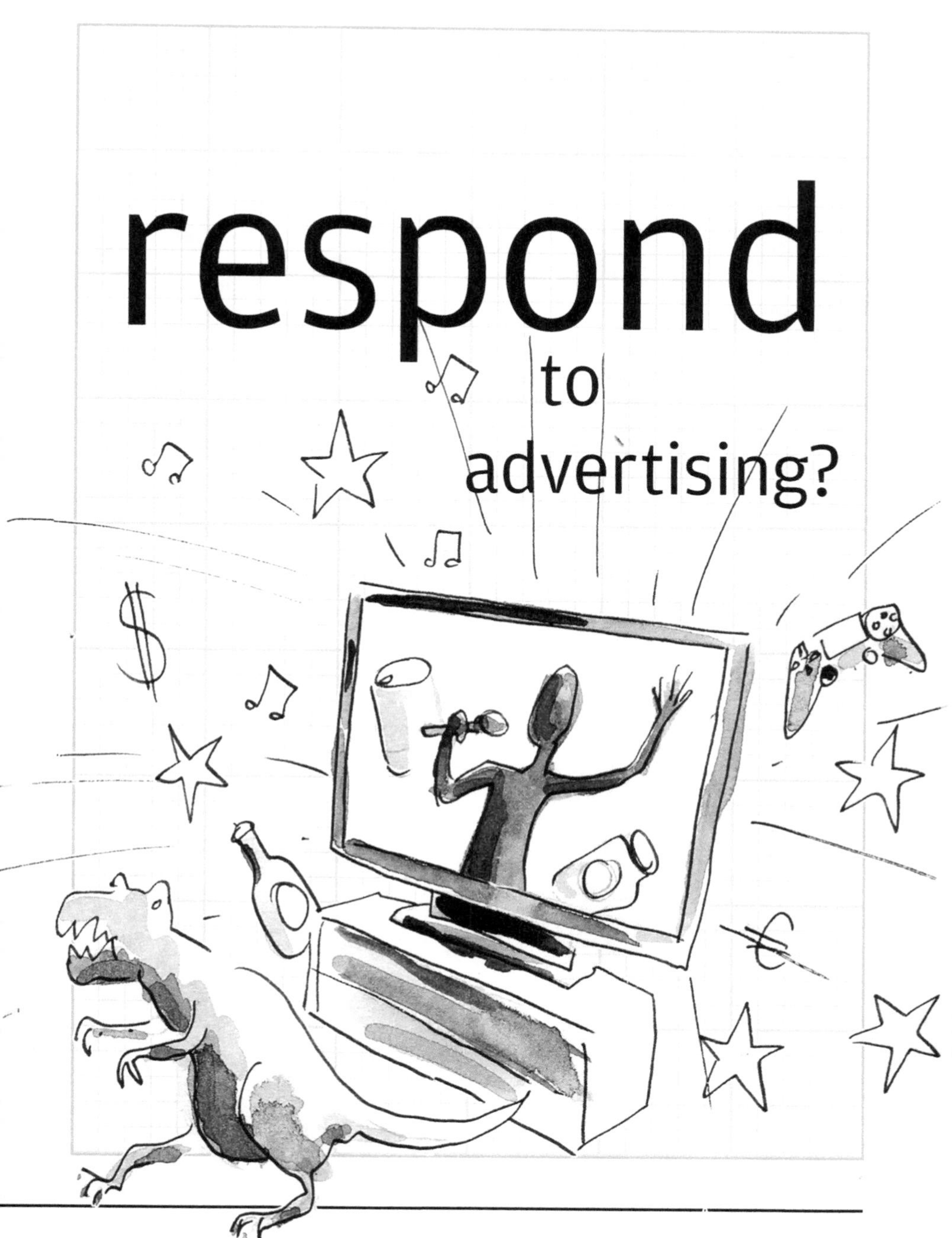

“

The only people who care about advertising are the people who work in advertising’

”

George Parker.
Confessions of a Mad Man.

How do people respond to advertising?

Many years back, ATV conducted an exercise with Leo Burnett Advertising. Creative Directors and Programme Producers were taken into homes under the guise of monitoring the use of electrical appliances. In reality, they were observing how people watch television – or not.

The viewers' behaviour was nothing short of appalling! Many did not pay full attention either during programmes or throughout commercial breaks. Some talked, some even left the room. They showed no appreciation or respect for the time, effort and dedication that had gone into creating the beautiful images on the screen. It was a horrifying experience for our professionals. It was also a valuable exercise because they were observing real life.

Thousands of books, articles, academic journals and studies have been published into how advertising works. Some great minds have dedicated lifetimes in the quest for truth. These are complicated issues with no easy answers and it would be impossible to try to summarise even a miniscule amount.

However, since simplicity and common sense are the mantras for this book, I am going back to one of the best explanations I heard almost forty years ago from Arthur Thompson (deceased). Arthur was a wonderfully insightful, plain speaking man who was media director of the Cogent Elliott advertising agency. He explained advertising effectiveness as a combination of strength of proposition, ease of delivery and latent product interest.

His simple analogy was that if you wanted to sell £10 notes for £1, and they were available in all newsagents, the only advertising you would need would be to whisper the information to one person on the street. This makes perfect sense. The proposition is irresistible, the product is widely available and our interest in it is extremely high.

However, if the £10 notes were only available from one store two hundred miles away or if they cost £9.90 then you would need to strengthen your proposition with a more persuasive message. You would also need to shout a lot louder and a lot more frequently.

This simple explanation leads me to suggest that we should conduct all analyses into effectiveness (and everything else for that matter) by product category to take into account levels of involvement and risk. The differences between buying a car versus a cola are so vast that it is crazy to use the same criteria when judging peoples' advertising responses. The other crucial factor is brand consideration that should be combined with category involvement for target identification and post-campaign analyses.

> **“The nature of the purchase decision has a strong influence on how marketing works, how strong its effects are, how we balance these effects and which strategies work best.”**
>
> Les Binet. Adam&Eve DDB
> Peter Field. Peter Field Consulting
> Effectiveness in Context. A Manual for Brand Building.
> Published by the IPA

Brand consideration is taken into account throughout Les Binet and Peter Field's excellent analyses of the IPAs Effectiveness Awards Databank. Not surprisingly, the more interested people are in a category or brand, the more effective marketing communications are likely to be both for brand building and activation.

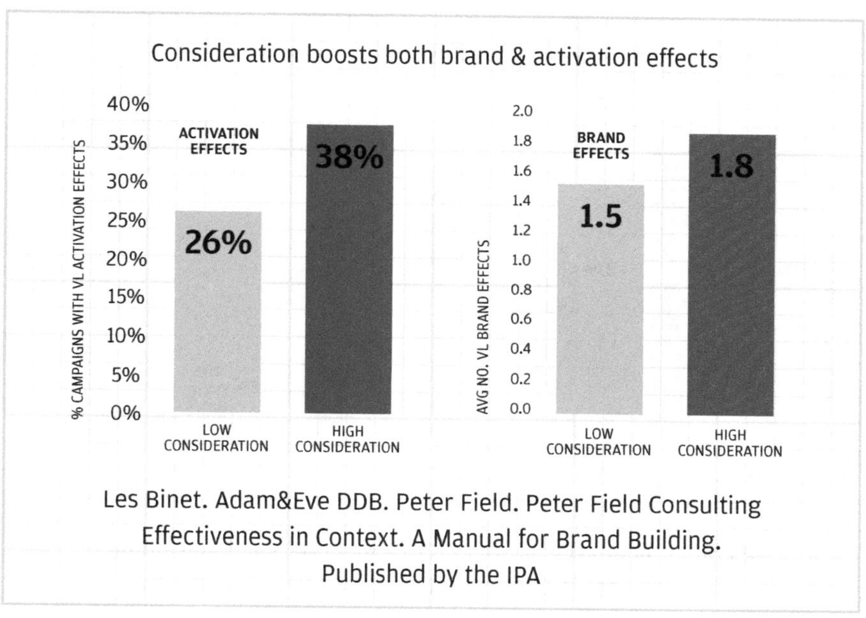

Les Binet. Adam&Eve DDB. Peter Field. Peter Field Consulting Effectiveness in Context. A Manual for Brand Building. Published by the IPA

What's more, high levels of consideration boost effectiveness and efficiency on every single metric measured in the analyses from sales and market share through to loyalty and profit. Put very simply, the more interested people are, the more effective communications tend to be.

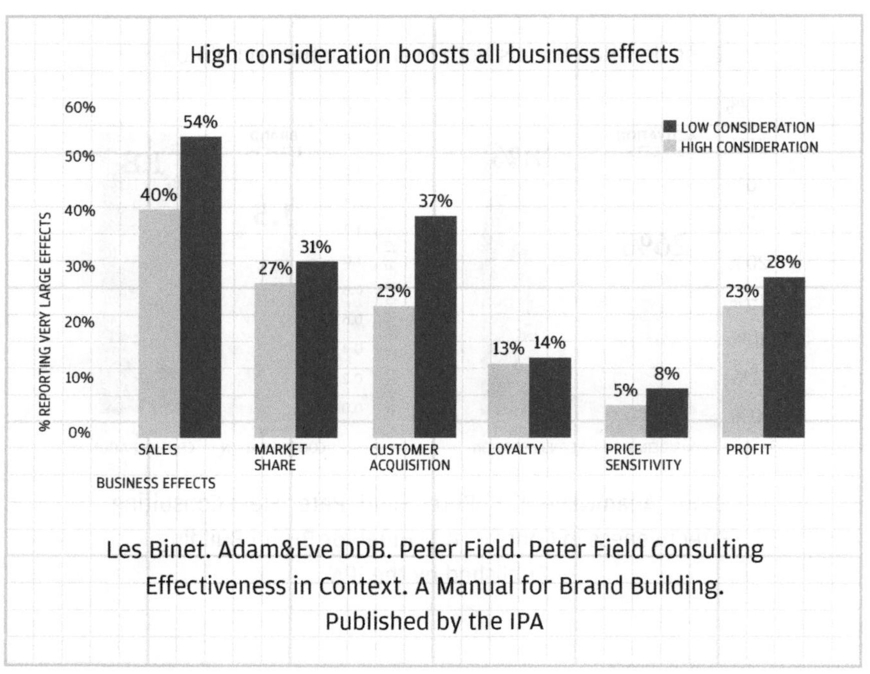

Les Binet. Adam&Eve DDB. Peter Field. Peter Field Consulting
Effectiveness in Context. A Manual for Brand Building.
Published by the IPA

I recently received a survey on behalf of a major retailer. It asked about my purchasing behaviour across a number of grocery categories one of which was instant coffee. They wanted me to describe how I felt 'emotionally' when making a purchase. It was an open-ended question and so I did.

I told them that I was 'beside myself with excitement. Not only was I going shopping for groceries but I was also going to buy instant coffee. Oh still my beating heart. I just couldn't wait for the time I would spend in front of the coffee shelves deciding which to buy. Would I treat myself to a luxury brand? Would I respond to a price offer? The anticipation was almost too much to bear.'

I ended by saying they were asking ridiculous questions (there were others) and asking how the hell did they think I would feel? Emotional? If I was as emotional about coffee as I became over the stupidity of the questionnaire then there may have been something to talk about!

The research was about low-interest, low-risk, low-involvement categories.

I spend a nano second in front of the coffee fixture. If I make the wrong coffee brand choice, I may be slightly irritated and will decide never to buy it again. But it isn't going to have the same impact as if I make a wrong decision when choosing a car, a computer, an outfit or a holiday. The implications are minimal. I just don't care.

Of course, even for everyday items we have differing levels of involvement. People have brands in their repertoire for each category and there are brands that they would never use. Whether the brand is on the consideration list has a strong influence on behaviour at the point of sale - we are blind to some brands. It is important to identify brand consideration for effective targeting especially in low interest categories.

Advertising can certainly have an influence although for everyday items it is likely to be subliminal in nature rather than overt. I like Byron Sharpe's summary that 'advertising works by creating and refreshing memories' ('How Brands Grow') although of course it can be much more complex than that.

We know that whether categories are rational or emotional affects advertising response. In rational purchasing categories (for high awareness brands) campaigns should be balanced in favour of activation messages than in emotional fields where the balance should be more in favour of brand building. Binet and Field have provided very useful indicators for different category types.

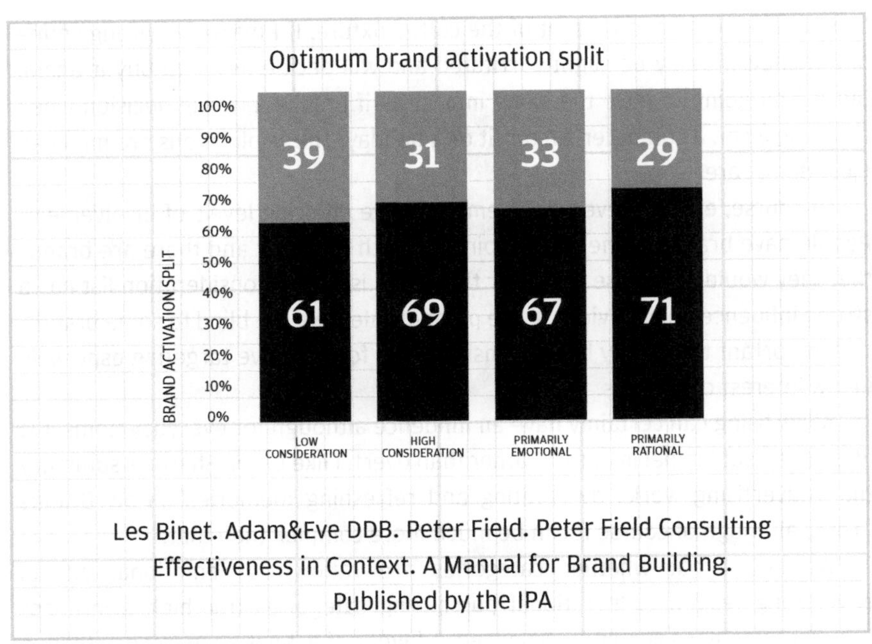

Les Binet. Adam&Eve DDB. Peter Field. Peter Field Consulting
Effectiveness in Context. A Manual for Brand Building.
Published by the IPA

Together with Binet and Field, industry gurus such as Simon Broadbent, Andrew Ehrenberg, John Philip Jones, Colin McDonald, Andrew Roberts, Byron Sharpe et al seem to have proved pretty conclusively that advertising works – often in mysterious and elusive ways.

> **“Advertising troubles both sociologists and financial directors. The former because they think it works and the latter because they think it does not.”**

Jeremy Bullmore.
J. Walter Thompson (1999)

Of course, in recent years, the advertising landscape has changed radically. There is a danger with the arrival of newer, lesser-known channels that we may become distracted and lose sight of the established basics when quite the opposite reaction is required. Social media make it even more urgent for companies to make sure the fundamentals are in place and then build their strategies from a strong foundation.

Some of the best commercial uses of social media aren't really advertising as we used to know it. Social media are personal spaces where people are at their most irritated by interruptions. However when it is useful information 'brought you by' (more like sponsorship) it can be not just tolerated but welcomed.

Proctor and Gamble cleverly use social media for BeingGirl which is less about product and more about addressing the issues faced by young girls from hygiene concerns to boy trouble. The site has received a small amount of criticism about product pushing but overall doesn't sell overtly and is praised for the information it provides on health and other relevant issues. Social media are perfect for this type of interaction: the audience is specific and the space is personal and intimate.

If we accept that the media work depending on the recipient's frame of mind, involvement, time pressure, motivations and the task in hand and if we further accept that category interest and brand consideration are key drivers of effectiveness, the surely these are the blocks on which we should build when constructing campaigns - and that goes for all media.

Are you

looking

for me?

“Nobody reads ads. People read what interests them and sometimes it’s an ad”

Howard Luck Gossage
(1917 - 1969)
Advertising Innovator and co-founder
of Wiener & Gossage Advertising Agency

Are you looking for me?

(Or am I looking for you?)

When actively seeking a product or service, we know what we want and of course we will take notice and maybe even interact with relevant messages - we are the seekers. Search is nothing short of a phenomenon in this regard.

As an aside, this is one reason why Amazon scores highly over Google for online shopping. With Amazon, people know what they want and tend to search for a category or go directly to a brand. It only needs to be efficient and fast. With Google, people are more likely to search for a subject or ask a question. 'How do I remove water stains from a wooden table?' would be a Google question whereas 'Wood stain-removers' would be the entry into Amazon. We ask the question on Google and then go to Amazon to make the purchase. Amazon users are further down the purchasing funnel.

But here's the thing. I don't think I know of many, or any, people who search for everyday products such as tea, biscuits or washing powder. Share of Google (SOG) analytics are wonderful for high consideration categories but are not relevant for the packaged goods sector. For once, there aren't enough data. Not enough people search for them.

It was much heralded that on-line media would be the panacea for all types of advertising but, to date, there is little evidence that they deliver for low interest categories no matter how accurate the targeting may be.

The reasons seem pretty obvious:

People want to be left alone when searching unless it's relevant to the task in hand.

"I hate it when I am looking for something on the internet and messages pop up that are totally irrelevant to what I am looking for. I think it is because they have data about me and want to sell me something. But when I am looking for something quickly I don't have time. It is annoying. It makes me irritated with the advert for interrupting what I am doing".

Female aged 32. London

Many people of all ages agree:

I find advertising on the Internet very irritating

	Net agree	Net disagree
Total	59%	8%
15-24	63%	10%
25-34	61%	10%
35-44	60%	10%
45-54	61%	8%
55-64	62%	8%
65-74	59%	7%
75+	41%	5%

Source: IPA Touchpoints 2018. Sample 51,903 adults

Advertising is less intrusive when people are browsing and relaxed

"I don't really like advertising at all but when I am just browsing around for things like travel or music then I guess I don't mind so much if an ad is there as long as it is something I am interested in".

Male aged 29. Whitstable, Kent.

They hate bombardment and re-targeting

"I searched for a black and white skirt, saw lots from different companies and bought one on-line. For weeks afterwards, I couldn't turn on my phone without seeing loads of black and white skirt ads. How many skirts do they think I want? I had already bought one. If these things are so clever, why doesn't it know that? It was very annoying. I was fed up with them".

Female 33. London.

And sometimes advertising is welcomed:

"I am very keen on jazz and find it really useful when information appears on the screen when I am looking at my favourite artists. I have been to events that I might have missed if I hadn't seen the advertisement on the internet. I would be cross though if they tried to sell me a car when I was looking for a jazz concert"

Male aged 44. Newcastle

There is little doubt that simple interruptive ads are a cost-efficient way to reach people but being cheaper shouldn't replace doing what is right. We deserve respect. It seems that advertisers want to beat us into submission when in reality the approach is having unintended consequences in forcing millions of people to use ad blockers and 67% of people to avoid advertising as much as

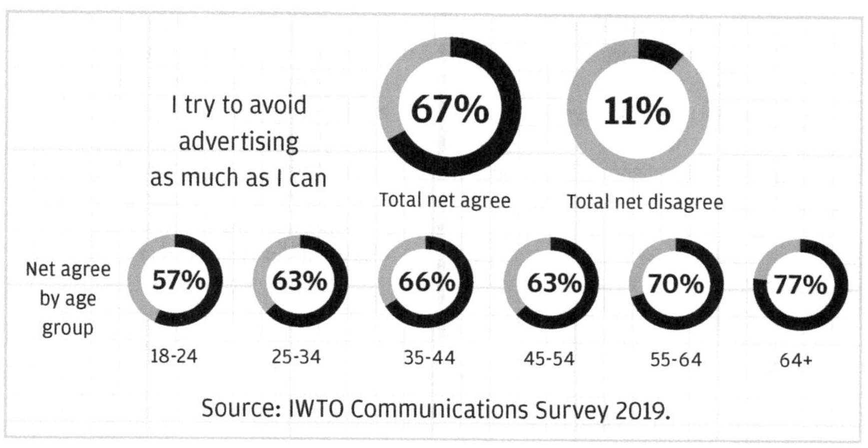

they can.

Of course there are times and places where advertising is more effective because it is timely and relevant. To maximise on these opportunities we need to consider frame of mind and purpose rather than only whether people are in front of the screen. How could we turn this into a way of thinking that combines task with mind-set and channel? I guess it might look something like this:

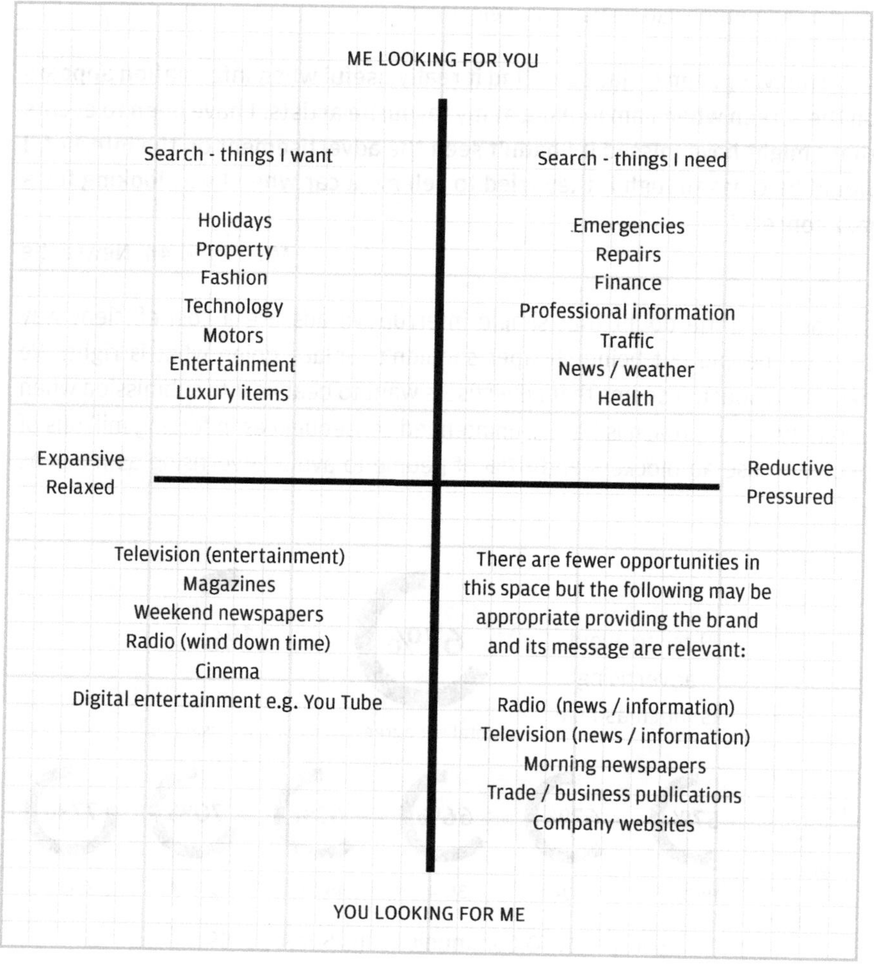

An expert view

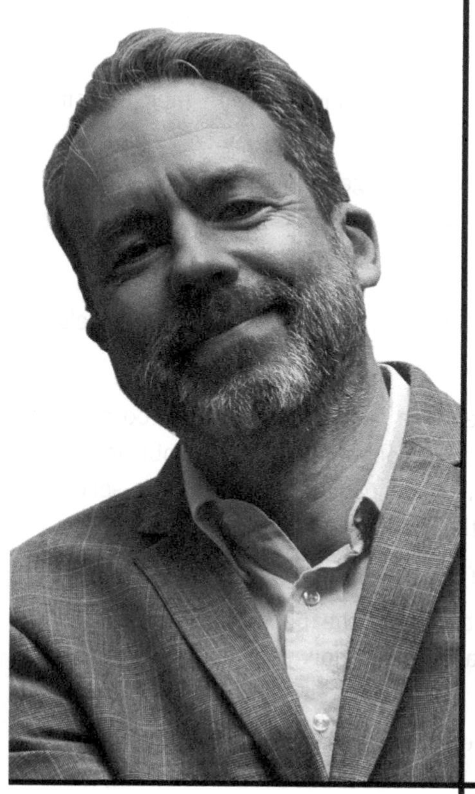

William Higham

Strategic Consultant.
The Next Big Thing

Q. What are the most positive changes you have seen in your business over the past 5-10 years?

A. In marketing/advertising/media:

- the democratisation of marketing / advertising from one to many to one with many.
- Brands are righty focusing more on communicating with their customers rather than shouting at them.

In trends/planning/strategy: CEOs today are generally much more:

- focused on the customer
- open to change / innovation
- willing to offer products/content/advertising across a range of channels

Q. And the most negative?

One of the most negative 'changes' is a lack of change! Still too much ad communication is focused on hipster 20-somethings. Some zombie industries (e.g. beauty, perfume, automotive, luxury) pay little more than lip service to the huge attitudinal shifts among their customers.

Q. Is advertising more or les effective than it was?

A. I don't know the financials but based on the polls I have seen, today's consumers pay less attention to advertising now and more to (sponsored) content.

This shouldn't be bad news for media companies. Success still hinges upon identifying a central idea. It's only the execution that needs to change.

Q. What part have digital channels played?

A. Digital is important as a communications channel but less so as an advertising medium. I have seen some fantastic content and Social Media campaigns but little advertising that I think works. It's too interruptive. Most people online are either researching product or idly browsing: an online ad gets in the way. My son learned how to 'skip ad' when he was just two years old!

Digital is a hugely effective medium for the distribution and communication of ideas but attitudes toward it are fundamentally different to those for traditional broadcast media. Campaigns that use it need to understand that.

Q. What are the most impactful trends that you are seeing in media behaviour?

A. The blurring of media channels: I can now access Netflix, YouTube, Chrome on my TV almost as easily as broadcast - a trend that will (and needs to) continue.

The recent shift towards complex media like video - and a counter trend towards simple media like audio (podcasts, radio) and print (books, magazines).

The counter trend is an attempt amongst consumers to reduce noise, escape Screen Fatigue and return to the 'safety' of tradition.

Q. What advice would you give to someone trying to understand what the future holds?

A. Spend time studying how attitudes are changing. Don't worry about what's exciting the media, the markets or the politicians, worry about what's exciting your customer.

New attitudes drive new behaviours: if you can identify which attitudes are changing you can predict new behaviours before they happen.

How? Multi-disciplinary immersive research (study sales, polls, box office receipts, ticket sales) to identify Change Points.

When something changes** (e.g. a sector/product type/market/ genre rises or falls) try to understand why it is happening and what happens as a consequence to:

- your customers' behaviour
- your customers' needs
- your company's distribution platforms, revenue models and sales
- other industries: suppliers to competitors
- society, media, retail and infrastructure

** Trend comes fro the Anglo Saxon word 'trendum' meaning a bend in a river: a trend is a change in direction.

Q. What advice to you wish you had been given when starting your career?

A. Think about what the client / customer wants and not what you can offer.

Q. What advice would you give someone starting out now?

A. Specialise! Everybody knows a bit about everything nowadays. To stand out you need to geek out - know a lot about one thing.

Q. What keeps you awake at night?

A. How to reconcile growing divisions within markets in particular the divisions between Progressives and Conservatives that are growing across markets globally. These divisions are reflected by polarised attitudes and voting preferences. It keeps me awake as a strategist - and as a citizen.

'Never mind the quality

feel the width'

'The Master and his Emissary'
A Fable
Source unknown

In his book with the above title Iain McGilchrist credits the origin of this fable to the philosopher Friedrich Nietzsche however this is disputed.

Whatever its source, it is the name of a mythical tale about a wise, spiritual master who rules over a land. The master appoints an emissary. He's a smart messenger and his job is to carry out the master's instructions and spread his wise words to the far corners of the land.

The emissary was bright but not quite bright enough to know what he didn't know - he thought he knew everything. He wondered what the master could possibly know that he didn't. After all the master just sat doing nothing while he, the emissary, did all the work. So he adopted the master's cloak and pretended to be the master. But because he didn't know what he didn't know, eventually the kingdom fell apart.

McGilchrist's book contains a great deal of scientific theory but it is also a commentary about modern, industrial societies. He argues that the right hemisphere of the brain plays the role of the wise master of our mental kingdom. The left hemisphere is the emissary.

He believes that we have grown infatuated with the skills of the emissary. We prize detail but scorn the bigger picture. He compares his analogy with the relationship between our brain hemispheres.

McGilchrist explains that we collect data and we know what they mean but to analyse them we need to feed them into a machine that is clever at routines but doesn't understand true problems or issues. The machine spews out a result that it also doesn't understand but we then take the result back into the practical part of our brains where the data live and believe we have found an answer.

He suggests that we have arrived at a place, and not for the first time in the West, where we have slipped into listening only to what the left hemisphere of the brain is telling us and ignoring what the right hemisphere could have shown us.

Just thought I would mention it.

“

Computers are like Old Testament Gods. Lots of rules and no mercy

”

Joseph Campbell.
American Professor

‘Never mind the quality, feel the width’.

‘Never mind the quality, feel the width’ is the title of an old British TV sitcom that ran for many years up until 1971. It seems like a good title for a section on data – particularly the big variety.

Beauty can be found in many types of data – big and small. A huge fuss has been made about the power of BIG data over the last fifteen years or so but it could be argued that we have been working with healthy sized databases for a lot longer. I am putting the emphasis here on ‘healthy’ as opposed to ‘big’.

In the early days of UK commercial television, AGB launched a research service called Television Consumer Audit (TCA).

Data were gathered from a continuous panel of ‘housewives’ who recorded all of their grocery purchases in paper diaries (respondents were far more amenable in those days). The brand buying data were then ‘married’ with the appropriate TV campaign ratings and the ITV companies used the results to ‘prove’ that TV advertising worked. We had no econometric meddling in those days.

I remember turning up at client meetings with long rolls of graph paper on which were drawn (by hand) coloured lines representing sales of the brands in the category, average price paid, weight of purchase, promotions etc.

At the foot of each chart were different sized blocks that represented the weight of television advertising expressed in audience ratings. The charts looked more like the London underground map but were surprisingly easy to read and told brand stories. And what powerful stories they told.

In the vast majority of cases, the weight of advertising at the bottom of each chart correlated beautifully with the shape of brand sales line at the top. You advertised on ITV, your brand flew off the shelves. Television advertising worked and the evidence was there for all to see. You could even persuade Financial Directors!

It was a doddle.

What's more, in those days ITV operated in a monopoly. There were no other commercial television channels so if you wanted to advertise your brand on television there was no alternative other than to buy your airtime from ITV. Audiences were huge. Viewers paid attention. All viewing was live. It was relatively simple to measure. It was easy to sell to clients. The money poured in. The expense accounts were generous. The lunches were long. Those were the days my friend.

I would argue that these were big data - or certainly big enough to advise on strategy in the environment as it was then. More importantly, they were meaningful because the data came from balanced samples.

> **A balanced, controlled sample of 1,000 individuals with a high response rate will always be more representative than 1,000,000+ customers drawn from an imbalanced, self-selecting or partial sample. Big does not always mean beautiful**
>
> Richard Marks, Consultant. Research The Media.
> Extract from 'The Big Opportunity' report commissioned by the IPA.

Confidence in the TCA results came from rigorous controls imposed by real people at every stage of the process from data collection through to interpretation.

Nowadays we have a much more sophisticated audience measurement than we did then. We also have more customer data plus surveys such as The IPA's Touchpoints and the long standing Target Group Index (TGI). They all provide credible, actionable information and, if used well, can help with strategic planning. Target groups can be identified in a myriad of ways: demographics, psychographics, geography, lifestyle, social behaviour, attitudes, buying habits and more. They are very rich sources indeed.

'Never mind the quality, feel the width'.

Nowadays, however, when we talk of BIG data it is often more about size than substance. I hear people waxing lyrically about the number of data points but a lot of it seems to be more about the 'what' rather than the 'why'.

> **"Big data problems are messy, often based on pattern-recognition rather than any theory of what causes what"**

> **"Statistically savvy people are sceptical of the hype surrounding big data"**

Tim Harford
Journalist and author of The Undercover Economist Strikes Back: How to Run or Ruin an Economy.
(Published by Little Brown)

Professor Steve Levitt, author of 'Freakonomics', made his name in his early days as a statistician working with big data sets and searching for the insights within. One would expect him to be a fan but he isn't.

> **"I think big data is highly overrated. It has promise but no-one knows what to do with it."**

> **"There's this vague idea that by having a lot of data you'll be able to extract insights that will change everything. But when you press people, the examples are almost always trivial."**

Professor Steve Levitt
Author of 'Freakonomics'. Taken from an interview with Tim Hartford

Seth Stephens-Davidowitz's book, 'Everybody Lies', is based on Google Search data and they don't come much bigger than that. The book is packed with fascinating insights into what we really think as we don't lie to Google when searching. Google Search is a truth God.

If you want to know the symptoms for measles, you are not going to search for mumps. If you want a recipe for beef you won't search for fish. It must the most truthful respondent database in the history of, well, respondent databases.

'Everybody Lies' is a fun, light and interesting read. The 'truths' behind prejudice, politics, racism and other elements of our societies are both interesting and worrying in equal measure. The truth about sex is - well, let me put it this way - it certainly opens your eyes on what people are really into (yes, yes I know - a lot more interesting than this but I will carry on regardless).

Interestingly Davidowitz talks a great deal about how we behave but does not try to interpret why. He is working with a colossal database and yet he expresses caution on how big data should and shouldn't be used. He suggests that even data of this magnitude should be complimented by smaller, more qualitative data to reveal the insights lying behind the numbers.

He's right. Premature extrapolation can be dangerous.

> “**The problem is this: the things we can measure are often not exactly what we care about**”
>
> Seth Stephens-Davidowitz
> Everybody Lies

An interesting case in point was the much-publicised news from Google that the spread of influenza in the U.S.A. could be predicted very quickly and cheaply. Google thought that they could use Search data to identify the correlation between what people searched for online and whether they had 'flu symptoms. It was going to be nothing short of amazing. Pharmaceutical companies would be able to gear up product supply and plan advertising campaigns to coincide with when and where the illness would strike next.

The following winter, Google's predictions overstated the number of cases by two to one.

The problem was that Google analysts were concentrating on statistical patterns. They were looking for correlation and not causation. This is common in big data analyses. Advocates believe that statistical correlation tells us all we need to know so models aren't needed.

An essay published in Wired magazine called 'The End of Theory', stated that 'with enough data, the numbers speak for themselves'.

This is "Complete bollocks. Absolute nonsense" according to David John Spiegelhalter, Statistician and Winton Professor of the Public Understanding of Risk at the University of Cambridge.

Figuring out what correlates with what is relatively straightforward. Figuring out what causes what is more difficult. If the reasons behind the correlation are unknown then we don't know what has caused it to be inaccurate?

One explanation of the flu prediction failure is that the news media were full of stories about imminent outbreaks that may have encouraged healthy people to search. Another possibility is that Google's own algorithm automatically suggested diagnoses of 'flu when people entered medical symptoms. Their symptoms may have been misappropriated towards 'flu when in fact they were suffering from something else.

Of course lessons were learned. As time goes by new techniques and recalibrations have been developed to prevent the same mistakes from being repeated. As a result there are many reasons to be positive and enthusiastic about the ease by which huge amounts of data can be combined and analysed.

Another much quoted example goes back much further - to 1936 - when a US magazine, The Literary Digest, mailed out 10 million surveys in an attempt to predict the result of the presidential election. After analysing 2.4 million responses (researchers - dream on!) they predicted a resounding victory for Alfred Landon over Franklin D Roosevelt.

In the event they were correct. There was a resounding victory. But it was for Roosevelt and not for Landon.

As if that wasn't bad enough, at the same time George Gallop had correctly forecast the result with a far smaller sample. Like Richard Marks, quoted earlier, Gallop understood that it is far more important to have a sample that represents the population than it is to have a dataset that is just big.

> **Continuous, non-intrusive data collection will become increasingly common. It's not yet of great value to many marketers because a) much of it doesn't show anything that isn't already known and b) the ability to analyse data (of any sort) is not as strong as it should be. Such data will become more prevalent. Today it is over-hyped**

Byron Sharp
Author of 'How Brands Grow'

My feeling is that relentless blind faith in data can be dangerous. Rigorous checks should be put in place to ensure the balance and relevance of the different data sets. More importantly, common sense questions should be asked at every stage of the process.

A young researcher at Mindshare, having analysed a big European database, told me that 85% of French women over the age of 65 go to the cinema at least once a week. Oh really? I don't think so. He argued that it must be correct as a computer analysis had produced the 'fact'. He showed me the computer screen as 'proof'.

Only when I asked him to think about his mother, grandmother and aunts did he concede that there could be an error. He was young. He knew nothing about the cinema behaviour of old women - let alone French old women. It's understandable that mistakes are made however, in every analysis, common sense questions must be applied. I hope that he learned a valuable lesson.

Data fusion was as much in vogue in the 1990s as big data are today. Senior statisticians had rigorously tested techniques to the extent that we had no doubt over their validity. Dick Dodson, then at Telmar, and I decided to test how far fusion could be stretched in providing media planning solutions. We produced an ESOMAR paper called 'To fuse or not to fuse'.

We wanted to know whether fusion would work in predicting all types of media behaviour? Would it work beyond standard demographics through to attitudes and social behaviour? Would it be appropriate for all types of product categories?

Our basic hypotheses was dependent on using a data source that included both product and media behaviour. The sample would be divided into two groups and then joined together again using fusion techniques. As actual behaviour was already known it would be possible to identify whether the fused data were accurate in predicting the actual behaviour of the respondents.

Various data sources were considered. In the event the TGI was selected as it is a large, single source, demographically balanced sample containing both media and product information. It also includes lifestyle dynamics and covers both fast and slower moving categories. The sample was around 13,000 in each group. Fourteen variables were used in the fusion.

The important element here (and I am sorry to be repetitive) is that actual media and product behaviour, lifestyles and attitudes are available for both groups. This meant that we could hide the data from one group and predict it from the fused data. We could then hypothetically 'lift the lid' to reveal how closely the fused data matched the actual results.

Without repeating the whole paper here, the analysis showed that data fusion could predict extremely well when the category penetration was high e.g. large circulation newspapers and big brands. It was far less reliable for lower penetration categories and also when lifestyle or attitudinal dimensions were added. This is not at all surprising. Lifestyle and attitudes often transcend age, class and sex so fusion doesn't work so well in these instances.

We found that the fused data were less reliable for analyses outside the standard fusion hooks that are biased towards demographics and product ownership. Media consumption predictions were more erratic when product behaviour or attitudinal dimensions were added.

This may be important today as clients seek to adopt new segmentation techniques outside standard demographics. Maybe a word of caution is in order. It is important to note that our analyses were conducted from one database with a balanced sample and one data collection method and yet we found that analyses were less reliable outside standard demographics. Fused data demonstrated accuracy for straightforward dimensions but presented problems when more complex questions were asked. What hope does that leave us in our brave new world of 'big' data sets with complex behavioural variables?

In searching for fresh approaches it is important to ensure that all the segmentation dimensions are represented in every database in the analyses. I would recommend a lot of rigorous testing before shifting from standard demographics wholeheartedly. They may seem boring and old hat but they just may work better than anything else on offer. I have conducted many segmentation exercises and then realised, sadly, that standard demographics could have explained most of the results.

This is far more important now because big datasets involve combining many research sources. All have different data collection methods, sampling techniques, business objectives and so on. This forces us (or should force us) to address various questions:

- How balanced are our digital behavioural datasets? Can we believe the geo- and socio-demographics that may be included and, if not, how can we segment effectively at even the most basic level to predict behaviour?
- How much weighting is required?
- Into how many territories can the data be stretched? Are they less reliable when criteria outside standard demographics groups are used as happened in our fusion experiment? Who knows?
- Is there bias lurking in any of the databases? Of course algorithms themselves are not biased but the data on which they rely can be. Implicit, often sub-conscious, bias runs throughout the human race. (Just look at the results of the Harvard Implicit Association Test – IAT – for evidence of racial bias within societies. Take the test. You may be amazed at your own responses).
- How rigorously are they tested?
- Who is doing the testing?
- Are they tested at all?

There seems to be a belief that big data are the solution for all marketing challenges just as digital media channels are the answer to all advertising issues. More intense interrogation needs to be applied to both. Machines don't (yet) know how to ask questions and algorithms cannot produce strategies that come from unique life experiences.

One huge advantage of today's planning tools is that they use real-time data that allows instantaneous decision-making. This is a fantastic improvement to the past when we had to wait weeks for survey results.

That said, at times there may be an advantage in moving at a slightly slower pace. Is fast always best? How much time do we spend thinking about each marketing challenge nowadays? Do we simply feed every issue into a machine and wait for it to spit out an answer that we then believe to be a solution? Do we believe that data hold all the answers? How often do we test our theories?

There are too many questions here but strategic advice should be given only when we are confident that we have the answers.

> “**Man is still the most extraordinary computer of all time**”
>
> John F. Kennedy

> “**Woman too**”
>
> Sheila Byfield

Big data offer masses of potential when we want to look at straightforward habits and, if balanced, they are nothing short of brilliant when looking at multi-dimensional behaviours. However, we need to go a lot further if we want true insights. Experiences from those who work with Behavioural Economics cite case after case of human behaviours that are unpredictable and which data would never be able to interpret no matter how many millions of points are present.

This is not an argument for one type of research or data analysis over another. Big data can provide information that you would never reveal through a focus group. They provide confidence and assurance through size, breadth and complexity. Qualitative research can be insightful but often needs quantifying. A marriage between them will always be more powerful.

In both cases, if research or data don't back up your gut feelings then you have to question why. There may be some genuinely new insights but, on the other hand, your analyses could be just plain wrong or it could be that your gut is having an off day.

It's always worth asking a question such as 'Does your grandmother go to the cinema at least once a week?'

> **If you torture the data for long enough, it will confess.**
>
> Ronald H. Coase.
> Essays on Economics and Economists.

An expert view

Rory Sutherland

Vice Chairman. Ogilvy.

Q. What are the most positive changes you have seen in the communications business over the past five to ten years?

A. A number of us (hat tip to Richard Shotton here) are trying with some limited success to stop us thinking of ourselves as being in a communication business at all. It is a self-limiting mind set. Communication is merely a means; behaviour change is an end.

Q. And the most negative?

A. The conflation of efficiency with effectiveness. This is not only endemic in conventional business culture but is magnified by tech culture. Efficiency is a useful frame of reference, but not an end in itself.

Q. Do you think that advertising is becoming more or less effective?

A. Entirely depends on your category and the behaviour of your competitors. But the ideological reluctance of many businesses to invest in advertising presents an opportunity for those that do.

Q. If it's more effective then what part have digital channels played?

A. They are valuable as is. But they would be more valuable if people used them more judiciously, without disappearing 'down the optimisation rabbit hole', as Mark Read calls it.

Q. You are clearly a fan of digital media yet you talk of the context being potentially negative because they are thought of as free. What do you think are the best ways to use digital channels? What types of advertising are most appropriate?

A. Lots of types of advertising work in digital. But it has not yet worked out how to transmit the kind of costly signalling necessary for major brands.

Q. Can behavioural economics and algorithms ever be friends?

A. Yes. As an aid to judgement, not as a replacement for it.

Q. What advice do you wish you had been given when you were starting your advertising career?

A. It isn't really a career. I have had lots of different jobs. That suits me fine.

Q. What advice would you give to someone starting out now?

A. Become good at two distinct but interrelated things. Everybody else is trying to be best at one thing.

Never mind the width

feel the quality

“

It is estimated that 12.2 million people in the UK will use an ad blocker in 2018 representing 22% of internet users’

”

Source: emarketer

Never mind the width, feel the quality

'Never mind the quality feel the width' entered the British vocabulary back in the height of the TV sitcom's era.

Conversely, the phrase 'Never mind the width, feel the quality' is true of good ads. 'It does what it says on the tin', 'Love it or hate it', 'Naughty but Nice', 'No I'm with the Woolwich' are all old slogans that filtered into our everyday vocabulary. There are many more examples although I feel that truly memorable advertising slogans emerge less frequently nowadays.

Most people would agree that Sir John Hegarty is one of the greatest creative geniuses of our time. His work is widely recognised as some of the very best as well as some of the most memorable and effective.

A case to validate my point is that, when asked in an interview by Campaign magazine to name some memorable ads from recent years, Sir John struggled and said he couldn't think of any that really stand out - although he did recognise that Marmite, Nike and Netflix are doing 'brilliant things'.

Nowadays we are told constantly that people don't like advertising and will do everything they can to avoid it.

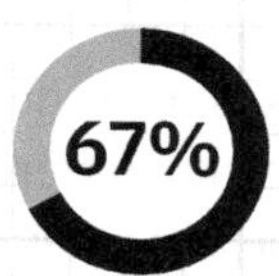

of all adults agree that they try to avoid as much advertising as they can

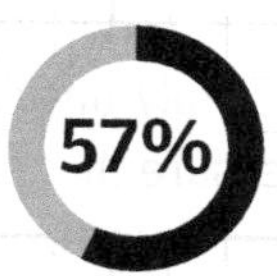

amongst adults aged 18-24

% = Net agree

Source: IWTO Communications Survey 2019.

Is it advertising per se that people don't want or is avoidance due to a lack of great, or even good, ads nowadays? Or are other factors at play?

> **"Most people ignore advertising because advertising ignores most people"**
>
> Bob Levenson

In the black and white world of the fifties and sixties when we had limited channel choice, no recording or playback devices and no remote controls, television ads were a novelty.

Over the years the novelty has worn off and many people try to avoid advertising. Why would they go out of their way to seek it out and interact with it because it appears in different formats?

Digital media are fast, efficient and nothing short of amazing some of the time. The big question with which we wrestle here is whether display advertising is at its most effective when screens are small, distractions are frequent and users are often active and task-oriented.

At its very best, online media may be a highly sophisticated version of the Yellow Pages that was an advertising only publication and worked well. Users went to it when they wanted something and searched for it. Just like Google.

Yellow Pages was predominantly lineage advertising (column width x lines per column) and so advertisers paid extra for ads with bold borders to draw attention to their products. It was all category-driven, classified advertising. However there weren't any holidays amongst the plumbers and no baked beans, coffee or colas anywhere. The task of the user and the tome-like print environment were simply unsuitable for brand-building campaigns. Of course we should work to ensure that our advertising stands out but when it interferes with the task in hand it is intrusive and irritating. In this respect the principles of Yellow Pages and search engines are one and the same.

One of the apparent reasons given for so much ad avoidance is the sheer volume of messages being thrust at us all day, every day. Walker-Smith claim we have gone from being exposed to around 500 ads a day in the 1970's to as many as 5,000 today. There are some that put the estimate closer to 10,000.

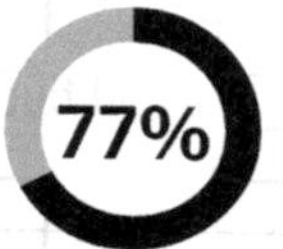

agree that there is more advertising now than there was five years ago

Source: IWTO Communications Survey 2019.

Is this really the way to look at advertising avoidance?

We conducted an experiment at Mindshare back in 2006 by giving people a counting device and asking them to click it when they saw or heard an ad but also, more importantly, had noticed it.

The results were rather revealing. OK, we may have the opportunity to see or hear thousands of commercial messages but the average number of ads noticed by our sample each day was 21. The challenge of course is to create cut through advertising so that it stands out from the 4,979 others competing for our attention. Every day.

A friend commented recently that she couldn't believe that I had had a career that had any connection with advertising as I am so intolerant of it. (She also, more worryingly, couldn't believe that I have children.)

But her observation on my career made me think.

I love advertising.

I still recall beautiful ads from years ago. I adore the sexiness of Levis Launderette and Swimmer, the cleverness of Audi's Vor Sprung Techniq and the simplicity of Nike's 'Just Do It'. I can still remember that 'Good things come to those who wait' (thank you Guinness) and can sing the advertising jingles to long-gone brands from the early days of commercial television. To be fair, the media were a lot less cluttered in those days but the ads were also a lot more memorable.

Maybe this is more about age than anything else but we used to discuss advertising in the past far more than we ever do now. Of course this is largely due to elements such as ad blocking, fragmentation and time-shifted viewing but it may also be due to the creative treatments just not being what once they were.

Perhaps it isn't advertising per-se that we are trying to avoid but obtrusive, interruptive, boring stuff in which we have no interest.

Maybe it would help advertising to be more memorable if the industry reduced its reliance on data for decision-making and brought back more human understanding and creativity.

“If the industry wants to survive it has got to lose its obsession with data and go back to its roots”

“Data is great at giving you information, giving you knowledge; but it doesn't give you understanding and that is its great failing.”

“Who says brands have to be on all the time? It's the digital companies telling you that. Wouldn't it be better to be on three of four times a year and do something great each time”

Sir John Hegarty

There is no formula for creativity. No algorithm can provide solutions that understand the weirdness of people whose behaviour is often spontaneous and unpredictable. No algorithm can understand how to ignite the emotional spark somewhere deep inside the individual psyche that will have a favourable influence on brand choice. Only people can produce stand out work that can do that.

Dave Trott, another creative genius, also supports Hegarty's view on doing less but doing it better:

> **Strategy is not about adding more stuff. Strategy is about taking stuff away. Taking away everything until there's only one thing left. One single powerful thought. One thought that's leaner and more powerful than the competition. That's why David Ogilvy said 'STRATEGY IS SACRIFICE**

Excerpt from Dave Trott blog posted on March 27th 2017

Please read Dave Trott's book 'Creative blindness and how to avoid it'. It is brilliant. In it he suggests that clients should be asked to judge ads by seeing them thrown across a table at speed because that's about the length of time that digital ads are seen. He exaggerates to make a point but it is a point very well made.

I see a day coming very soon when brand leaders will be saying that they went too far down the data route at the expense of emotional understanding, big ideas and effectiveness drivers. Some are starting to voice concern now. Some of us have been saying it for over a decade. I think they will recognise that they sacrificed emotion for numbers, took their eyes off the strategic ball and brand equity was sacrificed as a result. If we lose the desire to produce great, cut-through, stand-out, brand building advertising then the marketing and ad businesses have lost the plot altogether.

> **Creativity is the future. When we got a troubled brand we would go back to its roots – what made it? Why was this brand so successful? – and we tried to capture that again. It's the same with advertising, when it was great, what was it doing? We have**

to go back to that.
”

Sir John Hegarty

On the subject of creative genius, I came across an essay in 'Digital Advertising: Past, Present and Future' published by Creative Social. The book is a series of essays one of which is entitled 'What Would Bill Bernbach Think?' It's written by Sam Ball and Dave Bedwood.

Daniele Fiandaca, co-founder of Creative Social gave her kind permission to reproduce the essay in full for which I am extremely grateful. It puts into context the way we should think about advertising in any medium (pun intended).

What Would Bill Bernbach Think? By Sam Ball and Dave Bedwood

Séance transcript.
Kings Cross, London.
Present: Dave Bedwood, Sam Ball, Marie Baresford

Objective: To contact and seek the wisdom of Bill Bernbach, father of modern advertising, who died in 1982. Has the internet fundamentally changed the principles of advertising? If he were alive today, how would he approach digital advertising?

Marie Baresford: (slowly) Is there anybody there?

(silence)

Marie Baresford: Is there anybody there?

Colonel Sanders: Hello, I'm Colonel Sanders. Who is this?

Marie Baresford: Is anybody else there?

Bill Bernbach: Hello, Bill Bernbach here. Who am I speaking to?

Sam Ball: (slightly startled) God, hello Mr Bernbach. My name is Sam Ball and I'm here with Dave Bedwood. We're the creative partners of a digital advertising agency called Lean Mean Fighting Machine.

Bill Bernbach: What an absurdly stupid name, and what on Earth is digital advertising?

Sam Ball: I won't begin to explain the name, but we work in the world of advertising. Most of our adverts appear on the internet. Just to bring you up to speed, Bill, the internet is a huge connection of computers that spans the entire globe, enabling people to communicate, find out information, share photos, films, thoughts - all in an instant, anywhere in the world, without taking up any space or costing much money. Because people are spending so much time using their computers to do these things, advertisers now have another medium through which to talk to people.

Bill Bernbach: Have I been gone that long?

Dave Bedwood: Bill, we've got so many questions about life, death, God, the Universe ... but seeing as we might not have much time, the most important thing, we'd like to ask your opinion on is digital advertising. Do you think we need to rewrite the rule-book since the advent of the internet?

(long silence)

Marie Beresford: Hello, Bill - could you respond? I know you're still there.

Bill Bernbach: Sorry, I was just looking at an old book of my quotes. Well, it doesn't sound to me like you need to rewrite the rules, rather, brands need to go back to the core creative philosophies. I remember the advent of TV. We were creating newspaper, poster and radio ads at the time. The same conversations were ringing around the office: "Do we need to rethink how we go about doing great advertising? What is great advertising?"

Sam Ball: What were your conclusions?

Bill Bernbach: Let's put this into perspective. In the early fifties, only 10 per cent of homes had TV sets. By the mid sixties, this figure rose to 95 per cent. America was young and optimistic and there were exciting times ahead. The problem was that the old guard in charge of the advertising industry didn't know how to communicate with the new consumer effectively; they were still talking to people in a conventional way and treating them as idiots.

Sam Ball: Sorry to say, but some things haven't changed.

Bill Bernbach: Well the great art director Helmut Krone had a good analogy about this kind of advertising. He likened it to being sold to by a man on your doorstep. If he shouted or treated you like you were an idiot or talked down to you, you naturally wouldn't buy anything from him. We tried to write ads on the new medium of TV in a way that was thoughtful, treating consumers with respect and persuading them with charm and wit. The skills needed for that turned out to be no different than the ones we were employing with our best radio and press work. I would guess that these would be the same skills I would employ on your internet.

Dave Bedwood: I remember a quote you had from that time about the fact that it took millions of years for man's instincts to develop, so it will take millions more for them to vary. It's fashionable to talk about changing man. A communicator must be concerned with unchanging man, with –

Bill Bernbach: (abruptly interrupting) His obsessive drive to survive, to be admired, to succeed, to love, to take care of his own ......

Dave Bedwood: Yes, sorry, they are your words.

Bill Bernbach: I will stick by that. Every era has the same problems. We had it with advancements in mass media like TV but our philosophy was always to adapt your techniques to an idea, not an idea to your techniques. It looks like that might be even more important in your era.

Marie Beresford: Quite.

Dave Bedwood: We feel that the internet is the next step in what you were trying to do, Bill. Essentially, your ads were trying to talk to people and create a dialogue on their terms, but what we have is the chance to actually have a dialogue. People can talk back and get involved. In the past, however successful your communications, it was always one-way and passive. With our technology, we can create work that goes beyond anything a passive medium like TV could offer.

Bill Bernbach: I take your point, and to a certain degree, I think you're right. I would certainly see the internet as an extension of where I wanted to take advertising. We were trying to create a dialogue. Yes TV, print, posters are essentially one way, but to counter your point, I do think some of our best ads achieve this: they leave a gap for the consumer to fill in. By working out an ad, the consumer is interacting with it. I do see the power available today through the use of technology, but I'd warn you against believing that the core principles of advertising are not relevant.

Sam Ball: It's more that we think digital is different because the technology of the medium is so much more integral to how and idea can be expressed.

Bill Bernbach: But how do you go about creating the right strategy, tone, insight and message is exactly the same process if you wish to make a great TV ad or a great digital ad. How it is finally expressed differs because each medium gives a creative person different tools with which to paint the final picture.

Sam Ball: There is great debate at the moment as to who will own the future of advertising - the traditional agencies or the new digital agencies. What do you think about that?

Bill Bernbach: Well, at the heart of an effective creative philosophy is the belief that nothing is quite so powerful as an insight into human nature. What compulsions drive a man? What instincts dominate his actions, even though his language so often camouflages what really motivates him? This is the basis of any great advertising and, of course, has little to do with where or how the advertising appears. Wherever your consumer is, you need to speak to him in this way, via whatever medium. Whoever can manage to do that will own the future.

Dave Bedwood: We often say that a good joke in today's world could be seen in dozens of different media to a text message to Twitter to a press ad or on a phone, but what matters most is how good that joke is, To write a good joke takes a lot of skill and understanding of your audience. Without that it isn't funny, and no one will laugh, remember and pass it on.

(silence)

Bill Bernbach: I am sure that's one of my analogies but I will let it slide. It's a good point and relevant whatever year it was originally said. Yes, you have fantastic technology but it is only a conduit to the story, the idea. Those things, again, are powerful only if they are written in a way that touches the human psyche. The most difficult thing, as always, is not creating technology that allows you to share content; it is making content that is worth sharing.

Sam Ball: And how about the fact that people can now get involved in your advertising? Or ignore it altogether if they wish?

Bill Bernbach: How can they ignore it altogether?

Sam Ball: People are becoming more and more in control of their media and how they receive it. So, for example, with TV you can record it and play it back, skipping all the adverts if you like.

Bill Bernbach: How does the programming afford to be on air? Anyway, I think this is a natural progression, and to be frank, most of the advertising we used to have on TV was terrible – but that was because it wasn't made with the core creative philosophies I've been talking about. Whatever content you make today, as an advertiser you need to make sure it's good enough that the consumer wants to consume it. That, in my opinion, happens only when it's written from the standpoint I've laid out.

Dave Bedwood: How do you combat the rising power of consumers when they can use the internet to express their opinions, make their voices heard and damage an advertising campaign and product?

Bill Bernbach: If there really is two-way communication because of the internet, then I feel that there is even more need to write advertising that adheres to these core philosophies. Anything that doesn't will rightly become a victim of this consumer power. Surely, we will get less bad work ....?

Dave Bedwood: Do you wish you were in advertising today?

Bill Bernbach: Well, I'd like to be alive, so yes .... It does sound very interesting. My agency always wanted to create in the latest idiom. In my era it was TV; in yours, it's digital media. Like the sixties, it sounds like it's a unique time for advertising creativity. In my day, it was a change of mentality that allowed greater freedom and the letting go of old ways. Now it sounds like technology is provoking this creative revolution.

(long silence)

Bill Bernbach: I have to go now. J. Walter has got a couple of tickets to Johnny Cash and Buddy Holly's new band.

(silence)

Marie Beresford: He is fading ...

Dave Bedwood: Ah quickly, Bill, what's it like on the other side? What does it look like? What happens to you when you die? Do you get to play chess with Einstein? Are there animals in heaven? Is God a man? What was before the Big Bang? Is there life on other planets? Will the universe go on expanding? Is .....

Marie Beresford: He's gone ...

(long pause)

Sam Ball: Is Colonel Sanders still with us?

In the survey conducted for this book, respondents were asked how much they liked / disliked advertising in different media. Not surprisingly the majority of people claim not to like advertising. The percentage who dislike outstrip those who like across all media but strength of feeling differs significantly by medium:

% who like / like a lot advertising in:		% who hate / dislike advertising in:	
Cinema	21%	Pop ups	84%
Large posters	16%	Youtube	72%
Magazines	14%	Banner ads	61%
TV	13%	Direct Mail	61%
Search	13%	Social media	59%
Newspapers	13%	Search	44%
Direct Mail	10%	Inserts	45%
Inserts	10%	Radio	42%
Radio	8%	Blogs	38%
Ads in blogs	6%	TV	38%
Banner ads	5%	Podcasts	36%
Social media	5%	Cinema	23%
Youtube	4%	Large posters	19%
Pop ups	4%	Magazines	19%
Podcast	4%	Newspapers	18%

Source: IWTO Communications Survey 2019.

Advertising in traditional media is most liked and digital advertising tops the hate / dislike list. How many great ads can you recall in digital media? It's a question so often asked but how many great brands have been built through digital channels alone? As we saw earlier, why are the tech giants spending increasing amounts of money on TV, posters and dead trees?

We see a similar picture when looking at trust in advertising by channels:

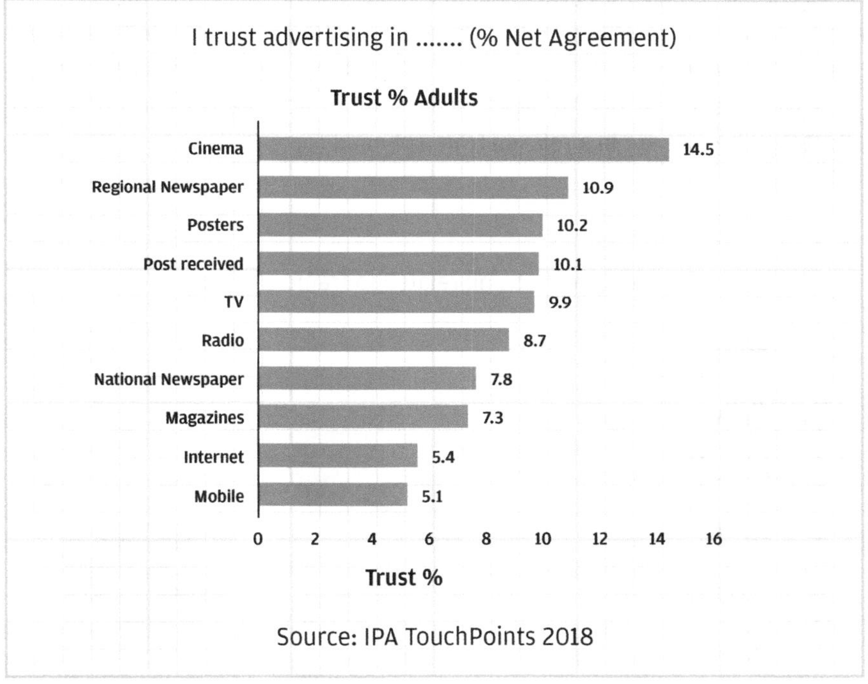

None of this means that digital advertising is ineffective but it should force us to think more carefully about the type of content we place in digital territories.

If we accept that the task (the reason why we are using the medium) and the time we have available drive our acceptance and response to advertising then surely we will also accept that great content deserves to be showcased in places where it will have the greatest impact.

A study by Kantar Millward Brown found that 16-19 year olds are at their most receptive to advertising when in the cinema. This should come as no surprise as the cinema is one of the few places where 'phones are turned off - or at least silenced and out of sight. Just for a moment, remind yourself of the environment from an advertising perspective. The audience is passive, the mind-set is purely expansive, every viewer has made an appointment to view, there is little or no distraction and the content often has undivided attention. Could it be any better?

Of course we can't put every ad in the cinema. It wouldn't be appropriate for every brand - audiences may not be appropriate or large enough - but we should use it as the ultimate environment for display advertising and work backwards.

If we accept that display advertising is more acceptable, and potentially effective, when we are in a relaxed frame of mind ......

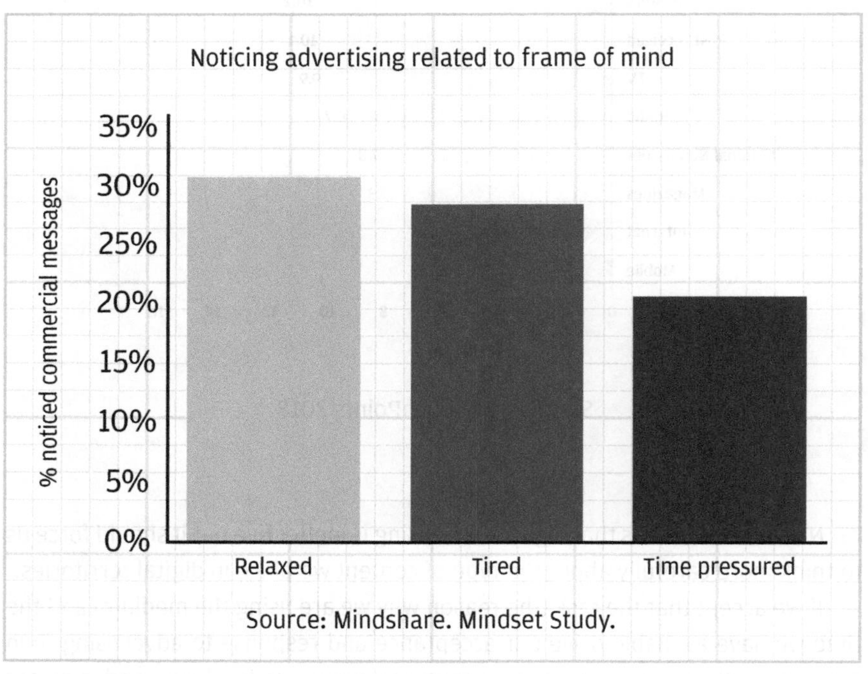

...... then it would follow that brand-building advertising will benefit if placed at a time and place where we are consuming absorbing content - irrespective of whether the vehicle is digital or not. The need state and the delivery method are perfectly matched.

Having said that, effectiveness across media may not be consistent even if we think we have achieved 'perfect' ad placement. Size of screen makes a huge difference on how we respond to both content and advertising.

I love YouTube but am confused with its strategy. I believe that they could exploit us more. My frame of mind is almost always relaxed and expansive whenever I request content on YouTube. I may not actually WANT ads, but they are far more acceptable than when I am pushed for time.

But YouTube often gives me the option to skip the ad after a couple of seconds. So that's what I do - always. I move on and never see which brand is advertised.

I can only assume that this option is offered because of the digital two-second measurement definition. This way I can be counted as an exposure and advertisers will pay for me. What a joke. To quote Professor Spiegelhalter again, 'it's absolute bollocks'. I can't believe that I used to whinge that a two-minute exposure to a page in print was insufficient to gauge whether advertising had been seen or noticed.

Do digital media really want the effectiveness of their channels judged by a two-second exposure? Please get real.

Why doesn't YouTube make me watch the ad in its entirety? I think they could do it. I am not suggesting long, TV-type ad breaks. The 'standard' that ads should adhere to needs to be short and hopefully entertaining to fit the environment but, as I mentioned, I am in a good frame of mind to see advertising - or at least probably won't object. I am relaxed and waiting for some of my favourite content. The provider is giving me something for free (let's not get into data collection and privacy issues here) so I am quite prepared to 'pay' for the content with my eyeballs.

It would be interesting to know if Youtube has undertaken research to identify the effects on audience size when people are 'forced' to watch fifteen seconds of advertising before video content begins. If it is negative and some leave, I would bet large sums of money that it wouldn't be anywhere near the number of people who, like me, tune out after two seconds and don't register the brand at all.

But hey, that's about effectiveness. Why would you bother about that when you can sell audience size?

Never mind the quality. Feel the width.

I am a big fan of speech podcasts and listen to a wide variety from a range of sources. My all time favourite is 'Hidden Brain' produced by NPR (National Public Radio) in the USA. After a short time into the programme there is an ad break. It's only for one or two brands and is very short. It is also for American business brands in which I have no interest and, normally, the voice-over is (in my view) intensely irritating. What could possibly be good about that?

Well, here's the thing; I don't mind a jot. I love the content of Hidden Brain so much and I am so grateful that they provide my chosen programmes at no cost (I don't even have to agree to terms and conditions!!) that I am more than happy to listen to a small amount of advertising - as long as they keep it short.

Why is that?

It's a simple a case of understanding the deal. I understand it with The Hidden Brain as we understood it with commercial television - they provided us with free programmes in exchange for watching advertising. Similarly with the BBC - they gave us ad-free content in exchange for paying a license fee. But with digital media the deal was never explained.

We were never told that Facebook, Google, YouTube and the like were all about data collection, data sales, data manipulation and advertising. We were so naïve. We thought that we were receiving unlimited, free content. We didn't realise (or we didn't want to know) that nothing comes for nothing. We believed Mark Zuckerberg when he said he wanted to connect friends 'to build community'. How stupid were we? We are starting to pay the price. It's an old adage but if something sounds too good to be true .....

Amid every positive aspect about our digital world - and there are many - this isn't the way that Tim Berners Lee saw it.

But I digress. Where were we? Oh yes.

The 'engagement' rules that apply to entertainment in digital media are the same as the rules that apply to entertainment in all other media:

Relaxed mind-set	+	Little or no time pressure	=	Advertising more acceptable

The rules change when we are communicating, shopping or searching:

More stressed mind-set	+	Time pressure	=	Advertising less acceptable

Strangely, in the on-line commercial world there seems to be an assumption that different rules apply. There is some crazy notion that catching us unawares by jumping out unexpectedly, uninvited and unwanted is going to enhance the way we feel about the medium and be more likely to respond to advertising. In reality it is having the opposite effect. This approach is annoying people across all groups - both young and old.

I find advertising on the internet very irritating
% in each age group who agree:

15-24	63%
25-34	61%
25-44	60%
45-54	61%
55-64	62%
65-74	59%
75+	41%
Total	59%

Source: IPA Touchpoints 2018
Sample: 51,903 adults aged 15+

"I hate it when ads appear on Facebook when I am talking with my friends. Can you imagine how you would feel if you were talking on the phone and an ad interrupted you? It's the same thing. It's rude."

Female aged 23. Newcastle-on-Tyne

Of course we will avoid advertising as much as we can if it is annoying. But perhaps instead of bleating about the evils of the blocker we should greet it as a wake up call. Maybe we should accept that if we don't respect people and if we continue to interrupt their conversations then they will dismiss us altogether. What a surprise.

Surely we should be working harder to develop an advertising culture that moves further away from the interruption model. You know - that's the one that was going to die when digital media arrived.

But instead of making it a priority to please audiences, we have used programmatic systems and algorithms to direct advertising towards places that cause more interruptions and an even greater turn off. I avoid people who don't treat me with respect and understanding in my real life, I am certainly not going to invite them into my digital life.

Of course none of this matters if people are responding in droves to the advertising they see online. But according to data provided by Kristina Volovich in The Marketing Blog, on-line click-through rates are 1.91% for Search and 0.35% for display ads.

WordStream research found that Facebook ad responses vary from 0.5% to 1.6% - an average of 0.9%. Of course click-through rates do not tell the whole story. Advertising doesn't always work through direct response but the response rates do seem very low.

Bob Hoffman has been banging on about this stuff most convincingly and for a very long time. In one of his blogs he quotes Professor Karen Nelson-Field of the University of Adelaide and founder of Media Intelligence Co who conducted a year-long study to determine whether TV, Facebook or YouTube delivered the best sales results.

A TV trade association funded the study so Bob was rightly suspicious over potential bias. However, his confidence levels were satisfied once methodologies had been examined thoroughly.

The overriding conclusion of the study was that there is a clear and direct causal relationship between attention paid to advertising and sales. The study found that people pay more attention to an ad on TV than they do to the same ad on YouTube or Facebook (there may be a strong argument here that the influential factors are screen size and the task in hand).

In the table below 'active viewing' means paying direct attention to an ad:

In an average ad second, TV commands more attention

	TV	YouTube	Facebook
Active viewing	58%	31%	4%
Passive viewing	40%	37%	94%
Non-viewing	2%	32%	2%

TV has about twice the attention of YouTube and around 15 times that of Facebook. This invalidates the claim that people 'tune out' TV ads or that a second screen has a strongly negative effect on the attention paid to television spots – Gary Vaynerchuk please take note.

'Passive Viewing' is defined as not paying direct attention to an ad but having it in peripheral vision. Facebook has a very high rate of passive viewing. This means that peoples' attention is often not fixed on the ad itself but on other things around it. While passive viewing has value, it is not nearly as powerful as active viewing.

'Non-viewing' is defined as neither paying visual attention to an ad nor having eyes focused near the field of vision.

Coverage - the amount of the screen that the ad covers - is another key component of effectiveness. One can surmise that the primary reason that television has more active viewing, and consequently more attention, is that the advertising covers 100% of the screen, thus reducing distractions, whereas the same spot on YouTube covers about 30% and on Facebook about 10%.

Added to this evidence, Thinkbox conducted a similarly revealing piece of work through Ebiquity and Gain Theory.

'Profit Ability: the business case for advertising' analysed over 2,000 campaigns across eleven categories and summarised that: "

- TV delivers 71% of the total profit generated by advertising, at the greatest efficiency (a profit ROI of £4.20), and for the least risk.
- Radio, TV and print are key to retail brands' short-term profit.
- TV creates half of all the short-term profit for travel brands.
- The majority of advertising returns (58%) occur in the long-term.
- Out of home, TV and online video deliver high long-term multipliers for FMCG.
- Out of home and TV have the highest long-term multiplier for financial services brands.
- TV is the safest investment in the long-term across all categories.

We know that marketers are under immense pressure to deliver results and justify every penny spent but given all the available evidence I am still puzzled. Here's the thing:

For years now Bob Hoffman, The Ad Contrarian, has been speaking in public, blogging and writing about digital advertising and the companies that control it. Time after time he has drawn attention to low advertising response rates, lack of transparency, fraudulent behaviour and unsatisfactory measurement. My question is this: if he is wrong, why has no one sued him?

It seems that no-one appears to be listening. Am I missing something? How much evidence is needed?

Let's ask Bob himself.

An expert view

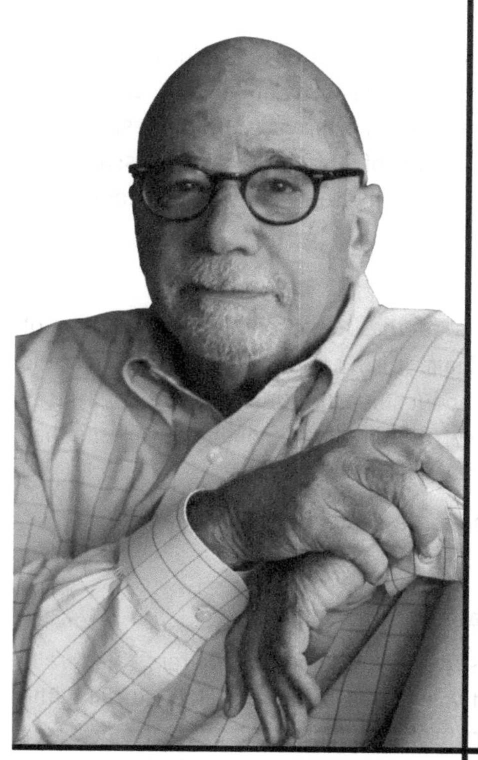

Bob Hoffman

The Ad Contrarian.
Chief Aggravation Officer.
Type A Group.

Q. What are the most positive changes you have seen in the communications business over the past 5-10 years?

A. The fact that large advertisers are starting to show some discipline and scepticism toward the torrent of bullshit the online ad industry has been feeding us is a positive sign.

Anyone with an open mind is re-evaluating a lot of the delusions we have been living under for the past decade: the avalanche of ad fraud; corruption; FBI investigations; bots; ad blockers; click farms; privacy nightmares; security breeches; election tampering; degradation of journalism; fake news; absence of transparency are causing intelligent people to ask if we really know what we think we know.

Q. And the most negative?

A. The most negative change relates to the collection and distribution of personal information about individuals. It is a serious danger to democratic societies. Advertising used to be about imparting information. Today it is about collecting information. To a substantial degree, online advertising has evolved into spyware disguised as advertising.

Q. Do you think that advertising is more or less effective than it was?

A. Less.

Q. What part have digital channels played?

A. Digital channels have played a positive role for some marketers - generally direct response marketers - and a negative role overall by turning the marketing industry toward short-term thinking and away from brand building. Digital channels have been substantially responsible for diverting our attention from creativity in advertising towards numbers.

Q. Your public speaking, books and blogs are very critical of digital advertising and the giant companies that control it. You draw attention to poor effectiveness, lack of regulation and unsatisfactory measurement. Is anyone listening?

A. Some are listening, most are not. The online advertising world is a cesspool of corruption, lies and confusion. It desperately needs to be reformed but so many people are making so much money no one wants to kill the golden goose.

Q. Are you seeing any signs of improvement in your core areas of criticism? In other words, has anything changed?

A. Yes in Europe. The GDPR is a first step but it is flawed by complication and confusion that are endemic to government regulation and bureaucracies. It needs to be radically simplified. In the States nothing has happened. There is more noise about the issues, but not much action.

Q. What advice do you wish you had been given when you were starting your career?

A. The only advice I wish someone had given me would have been to ignore the opinions of most advertising and marketing 'experts'. Other than that, I have no regrets. Most of the advice I got I ignored anyway. I'm a do-it-yourself kind of pain-in-the-ass guy who likes to figure things out for himself.

Q. What advice would you give someone just starting out?

A. Trust your instincts. Most of what passes for wisdom in advertising is just legends and rituals. Carefully study what the great ad people in your discipline did and ignore everything else.

Q. What do you think are the biggest threats to the advertising business and the people who work in it?

A. The biggest threats are:

1. Consolidation. Too much power in the hands of too few people.
2. Devaluation of creativity.
3. Consumer disgust with privacy abuse.

Q. Where do the opportunities lie?

A. The opportunities lie where they have always been - in the imagination and creativity of talented people. While the advertising industry has become obsessed with false goals, the true opportunities for success lie in finding and nurturing talented people.

A matter

of balance

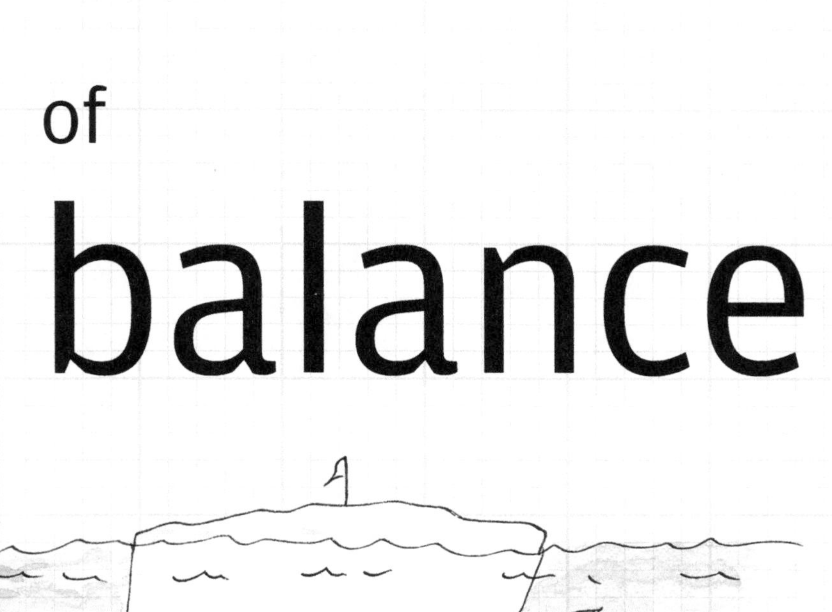

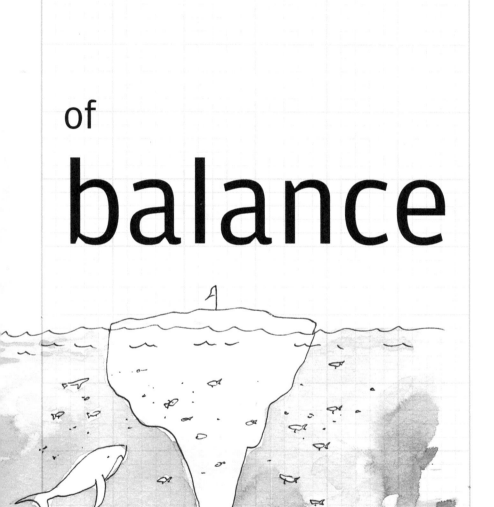

“

I have not failed.
I’ve just found 10,000
ways that won’t work.

”

Thomas Edison

A matter of balance

In the mid 1990s significant amounts of money were pouring out of advertising and into sales promotion. In those days it was known as 'above- and below-the-line.'

Marketing communities were delighted with the results. Sales increased dramatically with 'buy one get on free', money-off coupons and other discount offers. There was a lot of talk about television not being as effective as once was thought - how many times have we heard that since?

These promotions served the brand management fraternity very well indeed. They needed to demonstrate that they could increase sales in order to climb the corporate ladder. The sales uplifts from discounting gave them much needed ammunition. We called them '18-month brand managers'.

But this switch in budgets raised an important question: what would be the impact on long-term brand sales through short-term activation strategies?

To explore the issue Allan Breese, then at AGB, and I produced a paper for an ESOMAR conference. It was titled 'Should advertising spend be maintained at all costs?'

The work was extensive. We studied over twenty high penetration grocery categories and the dozens of brands within them. The analysis covered twenty years from 1973 to 1993.

We compared brands that had completely stopped advertising in favour of promotions, those who had switched a proportion of the advertising budget and those who had maintained their ad expenditure and had not reduced product price. We used TCA data for the analyses and the results were both revealing and conclusive.

In summary, the brands that continued 'above-the-line' advertising either maintained or increased brand share in the long term. Those who had abandoned advertising altogether in favour of promotions made significant short-term volume gains but lost long-term market share.

There was a further, unexpected dimension. The biggest long-term winners were those brands that had not only maintained their ad spend but did not manufacture private label brands. Nowadays private label products are high quality and are often brands in their own right. Over our analyses period they were seen as cheap alternatives. The group of winners in our analyses included companies such as Kelloggs, Pedigree Petfoods, Proctor and Gamble and so on.

Why is this important today? Because we are witnessing a similar trend with the movement of budgets from long-term, brand building campaigns in the 'old' channels in favour of short-term activation campaigns mainly through digital media. Of course there is nothing at all wrong with activation just as there is nothing wrong with price promotions. But what is the right balance?

The writing is on the wall for short termism.

The extensive work by Les Binet and Peter Field is great news for all of us.

Their analyses illustrate the rise in short-term thinking and, as a consequence, there has been a shift in balance in favour of activation for many campaigns.

As we saw earlier (P86) the optimum levels of investment in brand advertising for most categories is 60-70% with the remainder on targeted activation to drive short term sales. These proportions are consistent across both high / low consideration and also for emotionally-driven categories.

The balance varies significantly by category but the balance in favour of brand building in consistent.

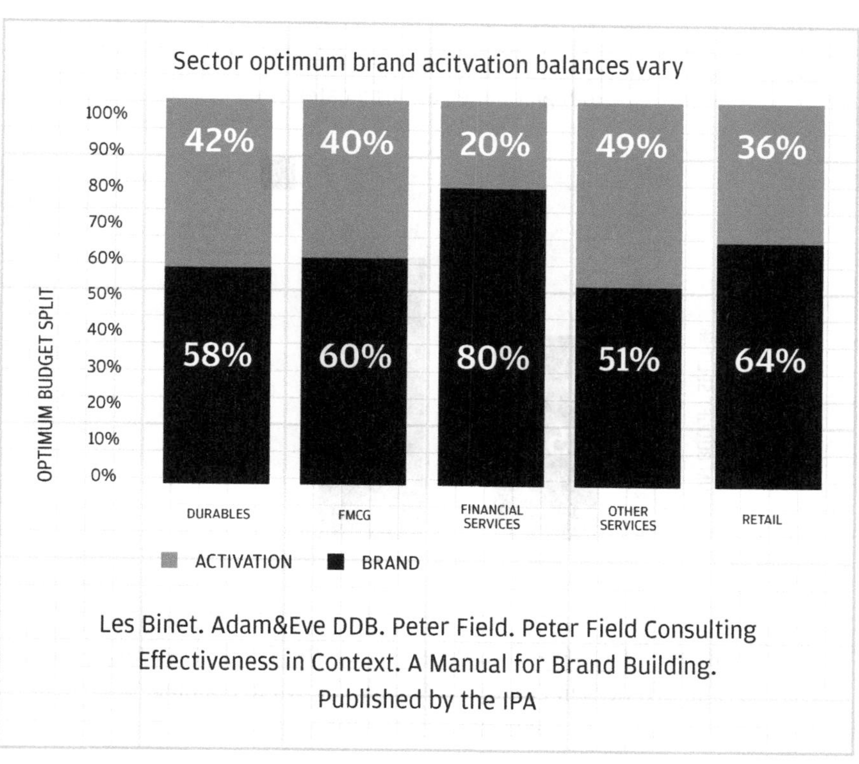

Les Binet. Adam&Eve DDB. Peter Field. Peter Field Consulting
Effectiveness in Context. A Manual for Brand Building.
Published by the IPA

> **“Short-termism is never smart”**

Effectiveness in Context
Les Binet and Peter Field

Of course the methods that people use to select and buy products has changed significantly in the last decade. Online research is a growing and important factor in purchasing. Sectors such as finance, motors, energy and technology are high research categories and it is therefore increasingly important to understand the optimum balance for online campaigns in conjunction with the older, more established brand building channels.

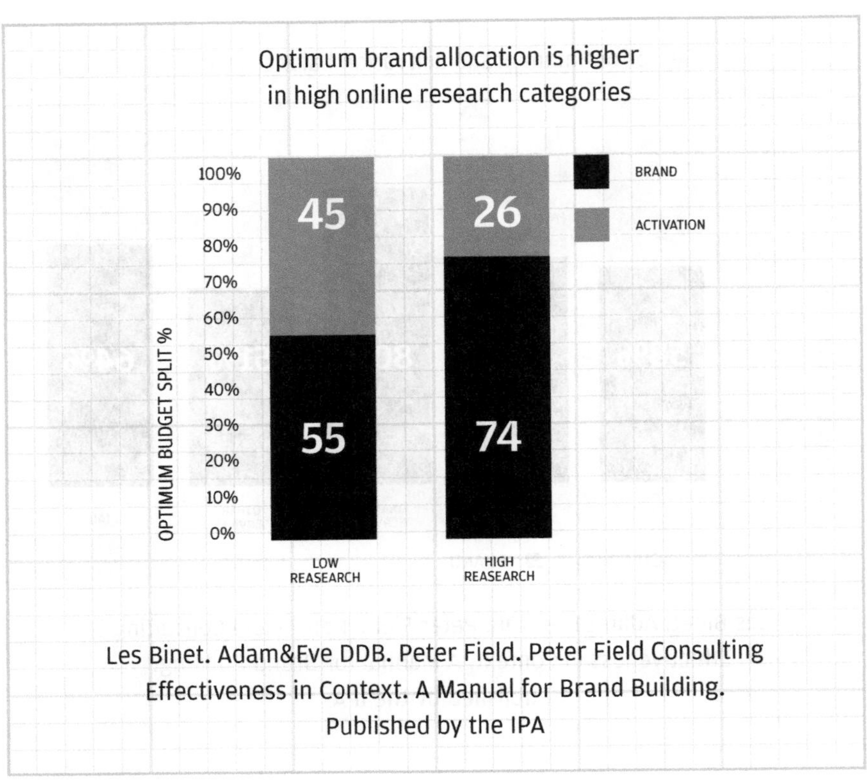

Les Binet. Adam&Eve DDB. Peter Field. Peter Field Consulting
Effectiveness in Context. A Manual for Brand Building.
Published by the IPA

The Google/TNS Consumer Barometer data measures online research by product category. This was overlaid onto 405 cases in the IPA Effectiveness database. Not surprisingly, highly researched categories are more likely to be those of high interest. If people like a brand they tend to believe the positive information that they see about it - favourability that has been built through brand building activities. No surprises there. I won't open up the can of worms of fake reviews - a dirty tactic even for the ad world.

> **Brand building is such a dominant force in effectiveness: it is not only essential for long-term effects, but also boosts short-term effects.**

> **Those who believe brand building is no longer important would do well to observe this.**

Effectiveness in Context. A manual for brand building.
Les Binet. Adam&Eve DDB
Peter Field. Peter Field Consulting

So just as I about to wave goodbye finally to this book and commit it to the publishers, The IPA have gone and published a report called 'Creative Effectiveness' which I can't ignore in the context of this chapter. Bloody typical.

It draws from over six hundred case studies and examines the correlations between creativity and effectivenss and also between creativity and efficiency.

It summarises that the correlations are weakening due to continued shifts towards short-termism and that activation-focused creativity delivers very little of the total potential.

Peter Field, leading effectiveness expert and author of the study said, "Despite our warnings, the misuse of creativity had continued to grow and the effctivenss advantage has continued to decline".

He goes on to say, "This report is a final wake up call for good sense before it's too late. We cannot afford to go on being complacent; left unchecked, the catastrophic decline in creative effectiveness will ultimately weaken support for creativity among general management. Money spent on creativity will become 'non-working' budget and will be cut".

How many more times do we need to be told?

Binet and Field, Ebiquity and Gain Theory and Enders Analysis have all conducted rigorous, highly credible analyses demonstrating the growth in, and dangers of, short-termism. They leave us in no doubt that a re-think is required that recognises ROI as a measure of efficiency but not a business goal in itself. The thought is not new but advertising must be seen as a long-term investment for business growth rather than as a cost.

Too often CMOs are thinking of ad investment in the short-term - a trait that used to be more prevalent amongst CFOs. There are close parallels here with the era mentioned earlier when budgets were transferred from mainstream media into price promotions. The strategy had negative effects on market shares across an extensive range of brands. There were lessons then. There are lessons now.

> “**An organisation's ability to learn, and translate that learning into action rapidly, is the ultimate competitive advantage**”
>
> Jack Welch CEO. General Electric 1981-2001

An expert view

Brian Jacobs

Independent Consultant
and author of The Cog Blog.

Q. What are the most positive changes you have seen in the communications business over the past 5-10 years?

A. Over a longer period it's clear that the arrival and evolution of the internet has changed everything – for good and ill! But over the more recent past, I would say that the growing involvement of major advertisers in media matters has been an overwhelmingly positive thing.

You could argue that advertisers should have been more engaged in how their money was spent years ago – but there's no question that the public involvement of large clients (like P & G) and their trade bodies (like the ANA and ISBA) has driven the agenda toward transparency, better and more open measurement, a greater appreciation of planning, more innovative ad appropriate compensation terms and so on.

Q. And the most negative?

A. Paradoxically, the obsession with media numbers over creativity is a major negative. We can now have numbers on everything and somehow we have lost the critical facility to distinguish the important from the irrelevant and the fake from the real. We seem to have forgotten that we're here to sell stuff, not to generate clicks.

Q. Do you think that advertising is becoming more or less effective?

A. Less – if we mean what might be termed traditional display advertising.

But I also think we are bad at defining what we mean by 'advertising' – anything with a brand name attached to it is seen as an ad. Yet despite that we live in an integrated communications world, we still operate in siloes. Why aren't the complimentary disciplines of (e.g.) PR, sponsorships, experiential all joined at the hip?

The reason is organisational – and that's no reason at all.

The consumer sees ads, the business has siloes. We need to be far better at true communications planning and execution, which in itself involves a greater degree of integration ad collaboration than we've managed so far in more than a handful of well-publicised cases.

Q. If you think more effective, what part have digital channels played?

A. I think less effective but the digital channels (by the way 'digital' is misleading - pretty well everything is digital) have been a boon for some advertisers. They have brought 'advertising' as a tool within the range of small businesses. Precision marketing using addressable techniques work very well for many companies.

But that's different from saying these things are the answer to every business problem. They're not. But then nor is anything else.

Q. You have had a long and varied career spanning advertising, media and research companies. What are the key lessons that you have learned from your experiences?

A. I have learned a lot but think that I would summarise as follows:

- Times change. Principles don't.
- It's stupid to say that one channel or a thousand makes no difference. It is true, however, that the basic principles of media still apply regardless of how many outlets exist.
- Ad campaigns work best when media and creative work together. Nothing beats a great idea placed in the most appropriate place at the right time.
- Separating media and creative was a bad idea but there's no point in whining about it. We need to create the working partnerships that existed between the best creative and the best comms planners.
- Agencies are potentially great places to work. They were fun, relaxed hard working places full of creative thinking and interesting people across all disciplines. Some still are. But far too many aren't - they're more serious, more corporate, less fun and, as a result, less creative. You need to have the right atmosphere for creative thinking to flourish. We are at risk of losing the ingredients that are essential for advertising to work.
- The business used to be about people - those in it and those we were trying to reach and influence. These days it's more about data, algorithms and meaningless gross impression numbers. It is sad. It's a major step backwards and needs to change.

Q. What advice do you wish you had been given when you were starting your career?

A. I was very lucky that I was taught to look around and learn the basics. I was exposed to all the disciplines in the agency so I could then decide what would suit me best. I was also advised to pay attention to the people you will be working with when choosing a job. As a result I was fortunate to learn from some of the greats like Norman Berry at Davidson Pearce, Dr Simon Broadbent at Leo Burnett and Sir Crispin Davis at Aegis.

Q. What advice would you give someone starting out now?

A. It would be the advice I was given: never stop learning. You really don't know what you don't know. Be curious and creative.

Seek out those prepared to offer you advice. In my experience, people are very generous with their time and are usually flattered to be asked. Meet and listen to as many people as you can, don't lurk in your office behind your desk. Good ideas can come from anywhere. Listen, absorb, apply and don't be afraid to do what Unilever used to call 'stealing with pride'. The great media directors of my day, Mike Yershon, Ken New, John Perriss and others knew about advertising, not just media. They were always looking to do things differently, to challenge convention.

Always do as you would be done by. It only takes a moment to answer a mail. Be polite and respectful. You are never THAT important or THAT busy. After all, Sir Martin Sorrell always makes sure that e-mails are answered within 20 minutes. And he's far more important than you.

Finally, never believe your own publicity. The loudest aren't necessarily the best informed (so says the blogger here!!)

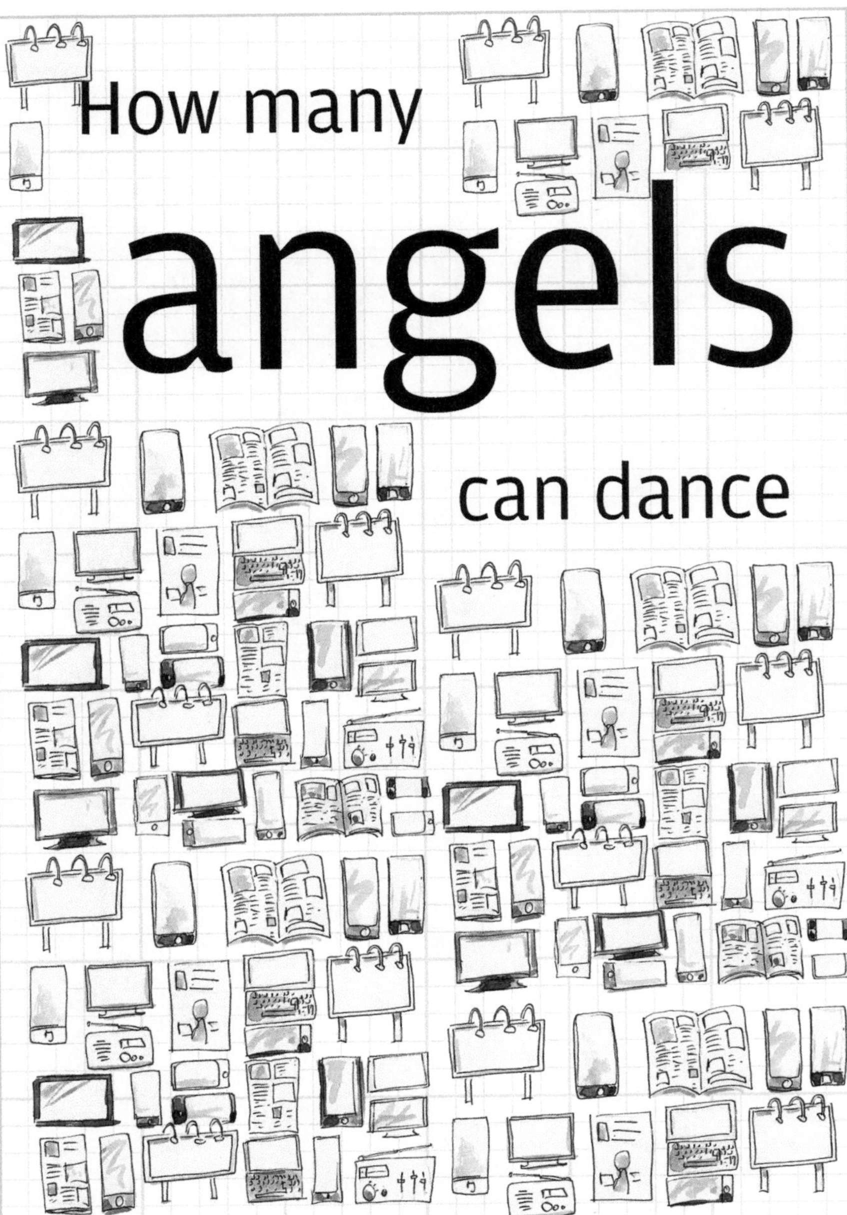
How many
angels
can dance

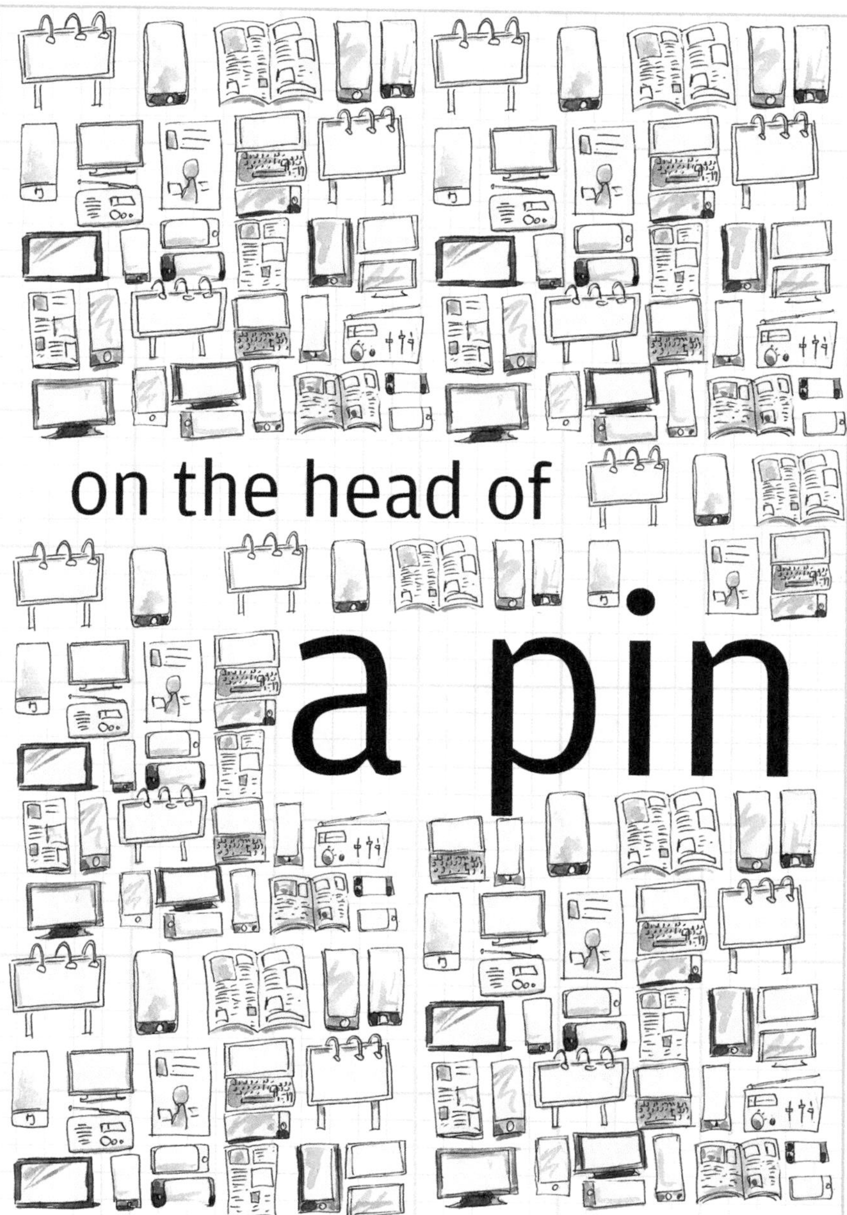
on the head of
a pin

> If you cannot measure it, you cannot improve it

Lord Kelvin

How many angels can dance on the head of a pin?

This is a difficult section to write and I have done everything to avoid it. I have taken holidays, completed piles of ironing and even watched daytime television (I never knew that 'Homes Under The Hammer' could be so compelling). Anything was preferable to tackling this crucial but thorny issue of how to measure media exposures and, more importantly, to understand their effectiveness in this media mayhem. Already I am reaching for the gin.

Let's start by looking at the numbers. A word of warning, I pulled some of these figures from the interweb so sources are varied and I can take no responsibility for accuracy. However the point is made that we are talking about a media landscape of monumental proportions.

Numbers relate to the UK unless otherwise stated.

- Fifteen national daily and eleven national Sunday newspapers are in circulation.
- There are fifteen hundred regional / local newspapers.
- The ABC (Audit Bureau of Circulations) audits four hundred and twenty two magazine titles.
- Wikipedia lists one hundred and fifty eight business magazines.
- There are nine national BBC radio stations, forty BBC local stations and over two hundred and fifty independent, local commercial stations.
- In 2017 there were four thousand, two hundred and sixty four cinema screens.
- According to Kinetic there are 425,687 Classic (paper) poster sites and 19,160 digital posters.
- BARB (Broadcasters Audience Research Board) measures 333 television

stations.

Clearly this next group could be just about anywhere:

- According to Netcraft January 2018 Web Server Survey, there are 1,805,260,010 websites.
- Google say that the web has 30 trillion unique individual pages. Just think about that number for a second.
- Google won't substantiate the number but it is estimated that Google Analytics is used by between 30 and 50 million websites. Interestingly that's a 20 million discrepancy but when we talk of this scale we just let it slide. Let's just say it is a hell of a lot.

We have had successful audience measurements for the first group of media for decades. To try and understand the billions of exposure opportunities from the second set is mind-boggling. My immediate reaction is that it is impossible.

Sadly, 'impossible' is not acceptable in this business.

Audience measurement research has delivered pretty well given the explosion in channel choice. The industry research bodies have continued to govern the shape, direction and quality of services and the UK maintains its reputation for delivering some of the highest quality media measurements in the world.

Industry contracts tend to be long-term and making change can be painstakingly slow but this may not be such a bad thing. It is tempting to want to measure everything and to measure quickly but it's difficult to predict what constitutes a real trend and what will turn out to be a fad.

The media business seems obsessed with minutia. Practitioners claim to need (want?) the behaviour of every individual by every medium for every second of the day for every day of the year. The only way to achieve this would be to insert a chip into everyone at birth. For some really creepy reason I wouldn't rule this out.

In the face of 'impossibility' surely we need to look either at the bigger picture and/or use the same technique as you would if eating an elephant i.e. carve it up into smaller, bite-sized chunks.

> **"Not everything that counts can be counted and not everything that can be counted counts"**

Albert Einstein

The jury is still out on the best methods to measure online audiences. It may be trite of me to suggest that it isn't exactly a bed of roses in the digital garden. The scale of online fraud is, allegedly, only exceeded by drug crime - it is estimated that only around half of digital advertising reaches a real person, Facebook have 'fessed up to fiddling (sorry that should be miscalculating) their audience figures, have claimed to reach more people in some demographic groups than exist and the debate continues over what constitutes effectiveness. It couldn't be better.

But please do not spend any of your precious time or energy worrying about these tiny insignificant, unimportant discrepancies. Help is at hand thanks to TubeMogul who came to my attention thanks to Bob Hoffman.

For the uninitiated, TubeMogul is a 'leading, independent, advertising software platform that enables brands to plan, buy, measure and optimise their global advertising'.

Hang on in here. They 'enable you to orchestrate sophisticated programmatic ad campaigns across digital screens, television and out-of-home channels from one platform'. They go on to say: 'Bottom line, our values inform strategies and help us stand for something. Click the video above to hear more'. There are lots of videos to click but when I tried to do so, on each one it said 'video unavailable'. This is a 'leading platform'. You couldn't make it up.

But put all of that to one side as we should all be indebted to TubeMogul. They have conducted some revolutionary research based on over one million streamed video ads and have concluded:

Wait for it ......

"Viewability matters when it comes to digital advertising. If ads are more likely to be seen, they are more likely to be effective".

So there you have it – we are saved. Just make sure someone sees your ad and there is a better chance that it will work. Phew – what a relief. I now have regrets though because I could have done so much better in my career had I known that.

On a more serious note, even if an ad is viewable it doesn't mean that people are engaging with it. But wasn't it ever thus? The business now seems obsessed with viewability (a word that doesn't actually exist) and click through rates.

In the course of preparing for this book – don't mock, I did some – I looked at heaps of recent research into what influences ad effectiveness in digital spaces.

Apart from the above pearl of wisdom that, I confess is difficult to beat, I came across these little gems:

- ads are less effective when placed in a cluttered environment'
- 'visual engagement doesn't tell you whether or not a campaign is actually working'
- 'a lot of ads are never looked at'
- 'if you don't have great creative your ad's not going to work'
- 'we should gain a deeper understanding into peoples' lives'

You could have knocked me down with a feather.

I suggest that the new generation of media practitioners takes a step back to yesteryear to examine the mountain of evidence on clutter, effective frequency, the effects of media environment, context, involvement and a whole host of other influences on the impact of advertising. Academics, advertising and media agencies, media owners and research practitioners have all contributed to this vast knowledge bank. There is tons of it.

Then take what you have learned and apply these trusted and proven findings to this fantastically exciting digital world that we inhabit. I promise you that all of the answers are there. There is no need to re-invent the wheel. You can impress your colleagues with your superior knowledge and concentrate on the really interesting stuff like strategic thinking and having fun.

> **I grow very tired of people not only reinventing the wheel but making it square because this is a new and exciting feature.**

Morgan Witzel
Business Historian

Of course things have changed and will continue to change. Your target audiences may be using different media, there is an attention deficit, ad avoidance is rife and behaviour is fragmented. But the basic drivers of advertising effectiveness rarely, if ever, change.

You may not believe this but there are two basic factors at work here:

- this game is still about putting persuasive messages in front of the most appropriate people at a time and place when they are likely to be most receptive and responsive.
- advertising works best when the message attracts attention, the advertising 'noise' (clutter) is at a minimum and your audience is exposed the optimum number of times.

When things become complex, it is often a good idea to go back to basics. You will find that some things just don't change.

This book is called 'In with the old, in with the new' for good reason. Do try and save that poor baby!

Of course we still have to count this stuff and measurement is faced with far greater challenges than it was ten to twenty years ago.

We are fortunate in our industry to have experts on these complex subjects and so it seemed a good idea to ask some of them for their views on audience measurement in the digital age. I am indebted to Andrew Green, Katherine Page and Andy Brown for their following thought pieces. It also means that I can finish the gin and go back to watching Cash in the Attic.

An expert view

Andrew Green

Global Head of Audience Solutions.
Audience Measurement.
Ipsos MORI.

We are entering the Fifth Age of Audience Measurement. It is an age where methodologies are being re-calibrated in response to a fast changing media environment and where the quest for total understanding of audiences is higher than it has ever been. It is also an era where politics and economics are far greater barriers to progress than technical concerns.

Looking back into history, we can say that there have been at least four key phases of development in audience measurement methods. The one we are entering now - the Fifth Age - is different.

The First Age was about counting copies sold, the Second Age about introducing radio and readership surveys in the 1930s. In the Third Age following the Second World War, meters were introduced and in the Fourth, starting in the 1980's, the people meter entered the fray.

But if it is different, it is not completely different. Many of the techniques and methods we can expect to feature in this Fifth Age are already in place: device-agnostic surveys, passive data collection, the integration of multiple data sources with traditional survey data etc. And there continues to be a role for high quality methods and skilled human practitioners in the process.

What may need to change is the attitude of the various industry players in favour of greater collaboration. Fear of change has been a great barrier to progress in implementing new methods - often exacerbated by the rising cost of measuring more platforms and reporting faster and more frequently. But digital technology has disrupted every business model and must be embraced, even though it offers difficult choices for many - including the need to invest in better measurement.

Co-operation amongst different media (e.g. sharing a panel equipped with multiple data collection technologies) offers one potential way of overcoming the financial challenge - as long as priorities can be agreed amongst the disparate stakeholders. Data science also has a far greater role to play in turning Big Data into usable insight. We have the methods: can the industry players come up with the money and the willingness to move ahead?

An expert view

Katherine Page

Freelance consultant specialising in technical advice and media audience measurement.

In a time when the same content is usually delivered across multiple platforms, no single technique can successfully measure media consumption across the board. Hybrid measurement is not new, but it is coming of age. Increasingly sophisticated techniques are used to bring together disparate datasets - some of the data are collected passively, or largely passively, and some by the more traditional route of interviewing respondents. A key development of note over the past couple of years, for instance, is the creation of so-called 'synthetic datasets'.

It is good news that there is so much data potential to work with, and increasing data science expertise within the industry, but the principles of sound audience research are the same as they ever were.

Understanding what each dataset actually represents, and its strengths and weaknesses, is just as relevant now as in the days when the debate was more likely to be about response rates than cookie deletion.

The key question is more pertinent than ever: how does the behaviour captured in a dataset relate back to a measure of people? After all it is people rather than devices that consume media and buy products and services. How many people are there? What sort of people are they? How representative are they of the population being measured not just in terms of broad demographics but the other lifestyle factors and interests that shape media consumption? 'Representative' can be a term used a little too easily: if only I had a bitcoin for every time I have been told that something was representative because the top line demographics have been weighted to match the population.

Ensuring that duplication of exposure to different platforms or media is represented appropriately is another key challenge in providing a measure of people when bringing together different datasets.

Ironically, often an old-fashioned survey is the best way to provide the context to 'bring everything together' by providing people-based benchmarks, establishment survey data and targets, demographic profiles or possibly a hub for fusion.

Combining disparate datasets will continue to be a major development area. As the complexity of the audience measurement task increases, so does the need for scrutiny ad transparency in order to produce currencies that are a reliable basis for the business decisions they underpin.

An expert view

Andy Brown

CEO. Kantar Media

Like the author of this book, I have extensive experience in audience measurement and feel that the industry is facing both challenges and opportunities created through new technologies and their associated economic structures.

I subscribe to the view that everything is measureable and the only barriers are politics and economics. I don't want to dwell too much on the politics but will draw on how technologies are influencing both media and marketing measurements in this rapidly changing and constantly evolving environment.

Our current challenges are not helped by the bewildering new array of metrics necessitated through the emergence of internet advertising. Impressions have transformed into viewable impressions, click through rates have developed into dwell times for both sites and ads and so on.

Much of these data can be described as large scale (big data) and deterministic (behavioural). The traditional media research models rely on high quality, often randomly recruited, samples or panels that use probabilistic measures and range in size from c1000 to c200,000. Any shortfall in scale is compensated through quality but the differences in these two formats are, arguably, the basis of the battle taking place around which is the best theory for media measurement going forward. In my opinion, there is ample room for both to work together and to compliment one another.

Soon we will see the world's first television people-meter measurement calibrated by large-scale set top box, or return path (RPD) data. Others will follow. This is challenging for the stalwarts of media measurement where probabilistic models have long reigned. In this new era of research, while the effective sample size for integrated solutions such as these will be that of the smaller probabilistic panel, the RPD component will aid calibration and provide data on small incidence viewing not picked up on traditional panels.

Television and video measurements are even more complex nowadays with the advent of more On-Demand, or Over The Top (OTT) services such as Netflix and Amazon Prime. The market will diversify further when more new players such as Apple TV and Disney join in. Some OTT providers have been vociferous in claiming not to need traditional viewing data from existing panels. They believe that their sole requirement is to measure how viewers engage with the platform and that assessment can be made through their own proprietary metrics.

Netflix, for example, shun traditional ratings claiming content can be designed purely from the performance of programmes and the actors who appear in them assessed through their own delivery platform.

They may have a point in an ad-free environment. These first party data are rich in content and come at a low cost when compared with continuous audience measurement panels. However, I would argue that it is remiss not to measure - or not want to know - what your subscribers are viewing when not viewing your platform.

What happens if subscriber or viewing levels begin to decline? Will the reasons be clear if there are a number of competitive platforms? How will you know who is eating your lunch? Early warning is essential to plan corrective strategy when problems occur and this requires integration with data on the broader market.

So perhaps the ideal solution would be to combine TV panel and subscriber list data to build a model that provides the wider context of both TV networks and (potentially) other OTT suppliers. We would then be able to integrate people-meter and RPD, blend probabilistic and behavioural sources and benefit from the best of both worlds.

Anything is technically possible in this day and age but ideal solutions in the measurement space will require political, economic and statistical compromise.

I guess the big question remaining is whether the industry is prepared to take the plunge.

Do unto others

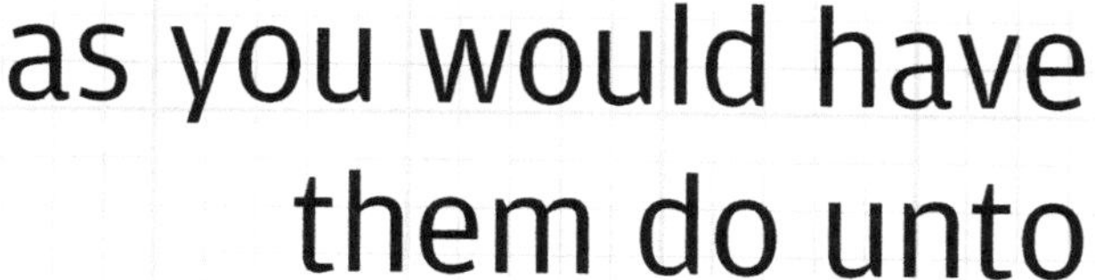

as you would have
them do unto

you

Luke 6:31.
New Testament

The Ant
A Fable
(or maybe not)

Every day the small ant arrived at work very early and started work immediately.

She produced a lot and was happy.

The Chief, the lion, was surprised to see that the ant was working without supervision.

He thought that if the ant can produce so much without supervision, wouldn't she produce even more if she had a supervisor?

So he recruited the cockroach who had extensive experience as a supervisor and was also famous for writing excellent reports.

The cockroach's first decision was to set up a clocking-in attendance system.

He also needed a secretary to help him write and type his reports and so he recruited the spider who managed the archives and monitored phone calls.

The lion was delighted with the cockroach's reports and asked him to produce graphs to demonstrate production rates and analyse trends that he could present them at board meetings.

To do this the cockroach had to buy a new computer and a laser printer. He also recruited the fly to manage the IT department.

The ant, who had once been so happy, productive and relaxed, hated this new system of paperwork and meetings which used up most of her time.

The lion came to the conclusion that it was high time to nominate a person in charge of the department where the ant worked.

The position was given to the cicada whose first decision was to buy a carpet and an ergonomic chair for his office.

The cicada also needed a computer and a personal assistant who he brought in from his previous department to help him prepare a work and budget control strategic optimisation plan.

The department where the ant worked was now a sad place where nobody laughed anymore and everybody had become upset.

It was at that time that the cicada convinced the lion of the necessity to start a time and motion study.

Having reviewed the cost of running the ant's department, the lion found that production was much less than before.

So he recruited the owl, a prestigious and renowned consultant to carry out an audit and suggest solutions.

The owl spent three months in the department and came up with an enormous report in several volumes. It concluded "The department is overstaffed ....."

Guess who was fired first by the lion?

The ant of course because she 'showed a lack of motivation and had a negative attitude'.

Note: the characters in this fable are fictitious; any resemblance to real people or facts within the Corporation is pure coincidence.

“

An organisation, no matter how well designed, is only as good as the people who live and work in it

”

Dee Ward Hock
Founder and former CEO of
the Visa Credit Card Association.

"Do unto others as you would have them do unto you". Luke 6:31. New Testament

Irrespective of your religious beliefs, the above is a very good code for how we should behave personally, socially and professionally.

I want to cover two aspects of how people are 'done unto'. First, how employers treat staff and then, how businesses treat customers.

First the staff.

I cannot overestimate how much I believe in training.

I believe that not training staff to help them perform and develop is nothing short of professional neglect. Lots of companies are guilty of this.

Before being allowed to visit even one client when joining the sales department of ATV (later to become Central TV) all new recruits in the ad-sales department spent time visiting the different parts of the company to learn how it all worked.

Time was spent in the studios – the fun part - and also touring the TV region. Several days were spent with the retail sales force selling brands into the grocery trade. Even more time was spent with research teams learning how audiences, programmes and campaigns were planned, measured and evaluated.

I had a similar experience when starting my career at Ogilvy and Mather. The first few weeks were spent with account planners, account managers, creative and new business teams. I worked on projects that helped explain the workings of an advertising agency. In the media department time was spent with planners and buyers across all different media.

In both companies, once properly on the job, I had a big picture understanding of the business. Consequently, I could talk far more knowledgably with clients than I would have been able to do with a one-dimensional view limited to my specific discipline.

In preparation for writing this, interviews were conducted with senior and junior planners from several media agencies. On the one hand I was pleasantly surprised. Media topics like effective frequency, recency, wear-out, environment, positioning etc. are not only still alive and kicking but have been re-shaped and enhanced through the availability of big, flexible data sets often operating in a live environment.

I heard that "while the major planning challenges have not changed, decisions nowadays are backed up with big data and algorithms combined with the availability of new platforms, predictive precision targeting and addressable advertising all of which influence channel choice and budget allocation".

While I am not sure that I fully understand all of that (and it's a hell of a long sentence), I am assured that this is all good news - especially when clients are placing an increasing emphasis on the use of data in decisions relating to their communications.

I did pick up a worrying issue in the interviews, however, and that was related to media agency structures and knowledge gaps. I was always critical that when digital media experts first appeared in our agencies, we sat through many presentations on how life (and especially our professional lives) would never be the same again. They were right. These sessions were essential for us to understand the changes that were about to take place and how they would impact on the commercial world. They were eye opening and valuable.

However, my criticism was that digital teams saw themselves as different, ahead of the curve and appeared to pay little or no attention to the other disciplines in the agency. I think that was a mistake as I have mentioned already. But that was well over a decade ago and this is now. Surely things will have changed.

I was somewhat surprised and disappointed to learn that a gap still exists between digital teams and the broader multi-channel planners. As one senior agency planner put it, "I feel that there is an increasing void between multi-channel planning and the digital planners. We sit in vastly different worlds. The challenge is how we bridge the agency talents. I believe that he winners will be the ones that can balance the two." Several others echoed his views.

More worryingly, I quizzed some junior media planners who seemed woefully inadequate at explaining even the most basic rules of how advertising works or what happens in other parts of the communications business. For example, a fair proportion had very little or no knowledge of the learning from the Les Binet and Peter Field work. These shortfalls really aren't difficult to address. New recruits should be given frequent training and be able to demonstrate knowledge and proficiencies on which they can be assessed.

Why not introduce an academy? Teach the basics, test the students, set projects (this can be handy as you can involve them in real-life client challenges), give awards and so on. A whole host of talents can be developed such as strategic thinking, presentation skills, leadership and team development. Above all, room should be allowed to harvest radical, creative solutions and ideas not bound by process and algorithms. It's also a great way to identify the stars of the future.

I am sure you are reading this and thinking that it's stating the obvious. Surely, most companies operate such training schemes. I thought the same but trust me, judging by the people with whom I met, it is far from universal.

> "**Hire people who are better than you and then leave them to get on with it. Look for people who will aim for the remarkable who will not settle for routine**"
>
> David Ogilvy

I have also been critical as to how many people working in agencies have never met the users of their clients' brands and their competitors. I think that agency management, and clients too, should insist that everyone working on a piece of business should gather insights through contact with brand users. I would go even further and use it as a personal performance measure.

And here's another thing .....

.... apart from the big media measurements which are still, in the main, policed by a Joint industry Committee (JIC) structure, agencies no longer seem to attach much importance to being involved in media research.

The UK's Media Research Group still operates successfully with its regular meetings and conferences but new research techniques are also presented frequently at international conferences such as asi and ESOMAR. And yet very few, if any, UK media agency research specialists are present nowadays.

Mike Sainsbury of asi runs very successful conferences in Europe and Asia each year. Both are well attended by an international audience of clients, media owners and research companies. asi provides very fertile ground for learning and exchanging views. Debate is lively with new methods and results presented and discussed. Mike informs me that no agency representatives from the UK have attended the European conference for many years although the event often attracts agency delegates from the Nordics, Central Europe and Russia. Clearly we Brits know it all.

Now I love an overseas trip as much as the next girl and spending three days at a conference attending corporate dinners and drinking late at night with colleagues is a very pleasant way to pass time. But that aside, I cannot overestimate the value of attending such events. Discussing the issues of the day with fellow professionals is incredibly valuable. I learned a lot and would go as far as to say that some of the most innovative research methods I have ever used have come from hearing about the experiences of other professionals at industry research conferences.

Sitting on industry research committees, being part of the discussion and driving quality standards were once essential parts of the research remit in media agencies. They should be again and I would urge practitioners to demand it and agency management to allow it. If you don't have a seat at the table, you don't have any influence on the direction of the research on which you rely and you sacrifice the right to criticise if standards slip.

You also have to ask yourself – would you notice?

Or would you care?

In this current, rocky period while media agencies are suffering from declining client trust, it strikes me that a return to holistic training, integrated structures and a greater focus on brand customers and research quality could go at least some of the way to address the problems.

C'mon guys. It can't be all that difficult. It may even make jobs more interesting, enjoyable and rewarding. You never know, clients may even thank you for doing it.

the7stars agency is the biggest independent media agency in the UK and since launching in 2005 has grown exponentially. They are winning awards, winning business and appear to have very satisfied clients and happy employees. I asked co-founder, Jenny Biggam, to explain the secret of their success alongside some other topics. Her reply is refreshing.

An expert view

Jenny Biggam

Co-founder of the7stars

Q What are the most positive changes you have seen in the communications business over the past 5-10 years?

A. I think that the opportunities for new advertisers and new business sectors to communicate effectively have been huge. Some of the biggest advertisers today (including Amazon for example) weren't advertising to any great extent 5 or 10 years ago. These advertisers are able to understand the effects of communications on their business in real time and it's great to see the flood into the ad market, including 'traditional' channels such as TV and outdoor.

Q. - and the most negative?

A. Conversely some traditional stalwarts seem to have fallen out of love with advertising - preferring price promotions and cost-cutting. Sectors such as consumer packaged goods appear to have cut back on advertising so significantly that it's hard to imagine their return.

Q. Do you think that advertising is becoming more or less effective?

A. I'm a believer in the long-term effects of communication and the research by Binet & Field that points to short termism resulting in lower profitability over time. However I think that advertising is now much easier to evaluate and optimise - and that greater knowledge and understanding drives effectiveness.

Q. If you think it's more effective, what part have digital channels played?

A. Digital channels enable precision marketing, better targeting and a better ability to deliver 'right message, right place, right time'. As consumers spend increasing time online, so advertisers find ways to reach them in digital channels. Sometimes I think digital channels' role in the communications mix is overstated for major brand advertisers particularly when considering the overall revenue trends. Many of the digital channels attract a very long tail of smaller advertisers, effectively replacing classified and / or Yellow Pages. For major brand advertisers their role is significant but often less significant than the overall stats sometimes suggest.

Q. In the time you have been operating you have not only grown exponentially but consistently achieve high scores in best company rankings. To what do you owe your success?

A. When we set up the agency we made it a core objective not just to build a successful company but to build a community where people love to work and create successful careers. It's a core reason why we set up the agency so its something we constantly check on and evaluate.

I think most media agencies value their employees and work hard to be great employers. The battle for talent is genuine - and talent really is a major differentiator for a media agency. I often think more so than for creative agencies because creative agencies can be judged on output (the show reel) while media agencies don't have a tangible product (nobody can see the comms strategy, or knows the buying rates) so quality of team becomes the most important thing for clients.

There are things that an independent privately owned agency can do that a big corporate network agency can't. We can take more risks and we can approach employee engagement in a much less corporate way. So I think we can actually beat the big agencies at this.

As we have grown it's harder to keep that close-knit feeling - so we work harder than ever to try and maintain our culture.

Q. You have broken the mould of agency structures by having the courage to introduce a different way of working. Can you explain the thinking behind your approach and the impact on your employees?

A. Our big thing is trust - we don't grade our team, or keep appraisal records. We don't ask them to fill in timesheets or holiday forms. We communicate openly and share even confidential information with the whole company. We even have a free bar with no rules about when it's open or closed.

By demonstrating such high levels of trust in our team, we find that they take more responsibility for their own output and take more initiatives to benefit the agency.

Q. What advice do you wish you had been given when you were starting your career?

A. Learn to type. When I started my career there were PAs to type for us and help put together presentations. Although we had computers I never learned, or taught myself, how to type. To this day I am a one-handed clumsy typist – and over the span of my career my typing speed must have cost me, literally, months of my life.

Q. What advice would you give to someone starting out now?

To learn and get involved in the industry in the broadest sense possible. I'm concerned to witness so many silos and specialisms in media agencies today leading to very narrowcast job specs and a generation of very specialist people, with little knowledge of the bigger picture. It's something we have actively tried to do differently at the7stars – giving people broader job roles and plenty of opportunities to learn about business as well as media and communication.

Squaring

the Circle

“

There is only one boss. The customer. And he can fire anyone in the company from the chairman down simply by spending his money somewhere else

”

Sam Walton
Founder of Walmart

'Do unto others' part 2: the treatment of customers.

In an era of increasing competition with fewer opportunities for product differentiation, one may have expected that companies would improve services and behave more courteously towards their customers.

People claim to want greater transparency, honesty, value and good behaviour from the companies and institutions with which they do business but seem discontented:

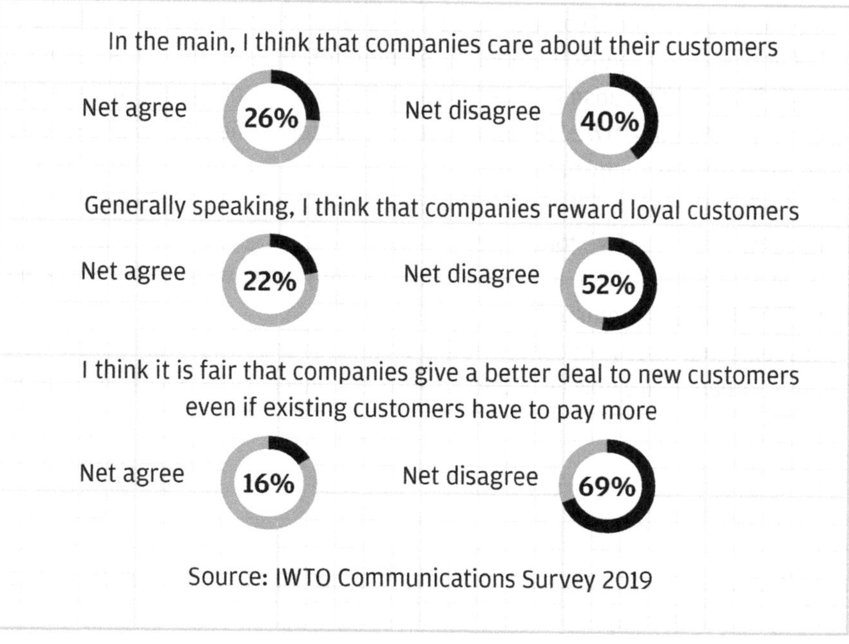
In the main, I think that companies care about their customers
Net agree 26%
Net disagree 40%
Generally speaking, I think that companies reward loyal customers
Net agree 22%
Net disagree 52%
I think it is fair that companies give a better deal to new customers even if existing customers have to pay more
Net agree 16%
Net disagree 69%
Source: IWTO Communications Survey 2019

It is estimated that 96% of unhappy customers don't complain, however, 91% of those unhappy people will leave and never return.

> **"Your most unhappy customers are your greatest source of learning."**
>
> Bill Gates

An American Express survey found that 46% of customers would pay 14% more for better customer service. Research by Zendesk found that 40% of customers would switch to another company because of a better customer-service reputation. Zendesk also found that 82% of customers who had switched had done so because of poor customer-service experience and that 55% of positive recommendations are made on service and not on product quality or price.

For obvious reasons, companies don't make a big noise over the volume of complaints they receive so numbers are quite difficult to come by. But, taking the UK's financial ombudsmen as an example, the volume of complaints received reached 400,658 in 2017/2018 compared to a decade earlier (2007/2008) when there were 99,699 complaints.*.

To be fair, there is a PPI effect included in the numbers but, even prior to PPI, complaints increased five fold in five years.

So if customer service is so important to the public, why don't companies move it higher up the marketing agenda?

It seems that instead of concentrating on the basics of what makes customers happy, companies are now all about purpose, enhanced experiences and stories.

---

* Source: Financial Ombudsmen Services Annual Report and Accounts.

There is absolutely nothing wrong with brands taking the lead, having responsibility and addressing societal issues. But it sometimes appears that the choice of purpose has no connection with what the organisation is about at its heart. Before jumping on any good-cause band-waggons, companies should strive to understand the reality of what is going on in the lives of their customers and their employees before making claims to be helping sort out deep-seated social problems.

If brands are going to support a cause then it should be endemic throughout the company. Everybody should be behind it. Employees are the best (or the worst) ambassadors for companies and brands. If every member of staff understands the cause or charity then the message can be amplified both inside the company and out.

I telephoned or visited forty companies from a wide range of product sectors covering retail, finance, motors, travel, technology, leisure, fmcg and fuel. I had first checked which causes or charities they supported. I am not going to name and shame here but fewer than half of the people with whom I spoke could tell me with which cause their company was associated.

Companies should be careful when jumping on good causes if they can't demonstrate genuine commitment. While people want companies to do good things for society in general and local communities in particular, they are sceptical about the motivations behind social responsibility initiatives:

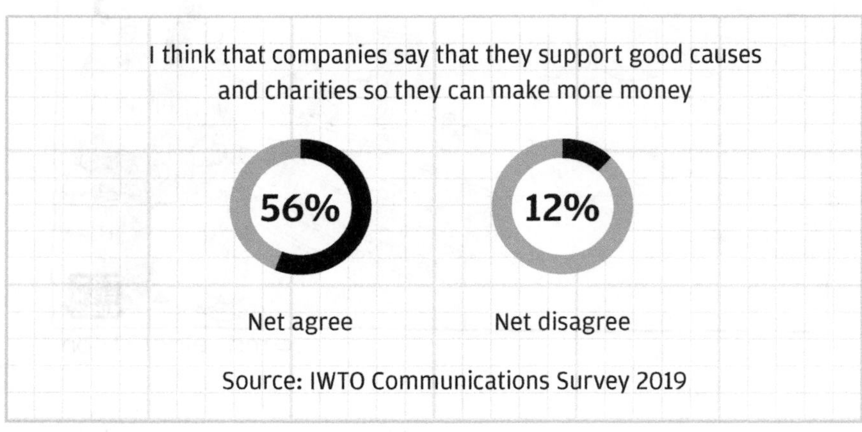
I think that companies say that they support good causes and charities so they can make more money
56%
12%
Net agree
Net disagree
Source: IWTO Communications Survey 2019

Gillette attracted a great deal of publicity when it told men that they should be more respectful to women. In a way, the 'The Best a Man Can Be' message appears to be a good fit with 'The Best a Man Can Get' and 'Toxic Masculinity' is certainly a serious issue that could benefit from mass publicity of a positive message. Reactions were both positive and negative. I was on the positive side until I discovered that Gillette charge women more per razor blade than they charge men which makes the message look superficial and demonstrates that having worthwhile purpose is not just about recognising an issue but that must stand up to the most rigorous scrutiny. Every brand must be transparent - particularly nowadays.

I recently read an extract from a Forrester Research and Accenture Interactive report. It stated that '87% of organisations agreed that standard experiences are no longer enough to satisfy customers'. Apparently this is because 'customers are placing increasing value on hyper-relevant, mindset-aware experiences that visibly add value to their lives.'

It went on to say that 'value is not being realised by growing bigger but adding meaning through unique and truly human-first brand experiences. In an increasingly competitive world, only the hyper-relevant will remain'. Apparently we all have 'shifting expectations'.

Maybe I am missing something but this sounds like a load of psycho-babble to me.

Of course people want good experiences and there are some categories where an average experience can be turned into something very special notably in the travel and leisure industries. Generally speaking, however, you find that people simply want what has been promised, to be treated fairly and with respect.

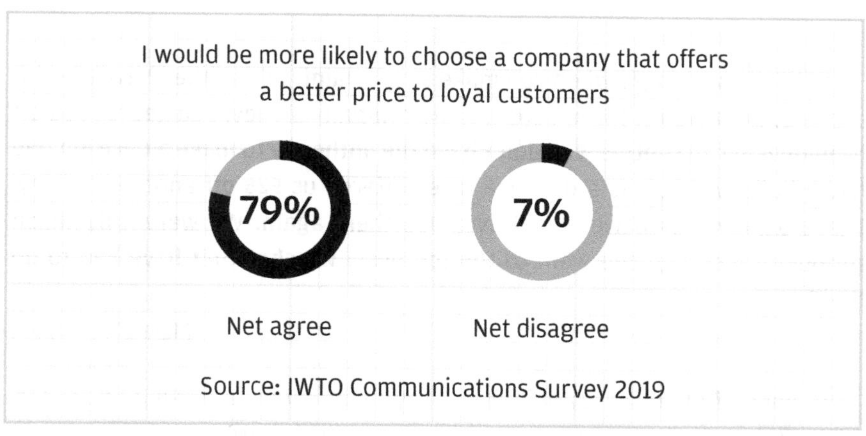
I would be more likely to choose a company that offers a better price to loyal customers
79%
7%
Net agree
Net disagree
Source: IWTO Communications Survey 2019

"I hate it when you want to speak with someone but have to wait ages on the phone listening to boring music or to advertising. I think they have a deal with the telephone companies to keep you hanging on for as long as possible so they can make more money out of you while they make you listen to their ads."

Female 47. Newcastle.

"I am really angry when I see an ad for a company that I am already with and they are offering a cheaper price for new customers. What about me? I have been a loyal customer but they give me nothing. In fact they charge me more"

Female 41. Newcastle.

"Companies just hope that you aren't going to notice that they have increased your costs when they renew your contract. If you ring up and say you are leaving them, they always come back with a better price. Why don't they give me the best price in the first place then I would stay? I always leave on principle"

Male 32. London.

"The worst thing is when you make a complaint. I think they have a script and they get a bonus for not costing the company money. You get fobbed off by people in call centres who don't have the authority to make a decision. We had a holiday that was a disgrace. They offered us £25 off another holiday. That's a joke - as if we would ever use them again. We were only taken seriously when my wife went to the top boss. We shouldn't have had to do that"

Male 37. London.

In none of my research did anyone say that they were looking for 'hyper-relevant, human first experiences'. All they want is fair treatment in exchange for their business. Above all they want to speak to people who act as if they care about the customer and have the authority to address problems.

There is a correlation between how well businesses treat staff and then how well the staff treat customers. People can detect when employees are unhappy and not empowered to deal with customer issues. They give poor service and don't have any motivation to walk the extra mile. Why should they if not appreciated or rewarded?

It is interesting that Amazon is rated top when it comes to customer service and yet has a shocking reputation for the way it treats staff. Maybe this says more about us than it does about Amazon. The customer service is so good that we turn a blind eye to what is going on behind the scenes. Shame on us.

I wish I had a fiver for every time I have heard a CEO banging on about 'putting the customer at the heart of everything we do'. You don't PUT the customer at the heart. They ARE at the heart of everything you do. Give me strength.

When David Ogilvy set up his agency he wrote a mission statement that differs from any other I have seen and possibly from any other ever written. This is only a small part of it and I have paraphrased but you will get the gist. It goes along the lines of:

I want to build a business where people are happy because if people are happy they will do better work and if they do better work we will win more business.

How many mission statements have you come across that begin with 'I want happy employees' or 'I want happy customers'?

> **"Customer delight is a more powerful objective than shareholder value ... if you take care of customers, shareholders will be drawn along for a very nice ride. The opposite is simply not true; if you try to take care of shareholders, customers don't benefit, and, ironically, shareholders don't get very far either"**
>
> Roger Martin
> Fixing the Game

Almost every major business today operates with an emphasis on shareholder value. This is both important and understandable but, with too much emphasis in one direction, innovation, creativity and entrepreneurship can be strangled. It sometimes appears that many companies have lost sight of what is really important to their staff and their customers.

It's another case of short-term thinking and, as in most examples of short termism, the effects are not visible immediately but become evident in the longer-term when it may be difficult, costly or simply too late to address them.

> **A business that makes nothing but money is a poor business.**
>
> Henry Ford

Measuring customer satisfaction can be a tricky issue. I don't know about you but I am fed up of being asked constantly what I think (and this is from someone who had a career in research!) Nowadays I am asked to rate everything I do. I can understand being asked for feedback on big ticket items such as cars and holidays but when a waiter in a hotel brought me a gin and tonic and a survey I almost threw it at him – that's the survey, not the gin.

Customer satisfaction is complex to measure. I experimented with some research concepts and, as I see it there are three main factors that apply to all categories. Each of the factors has component parts (weighted) and the weighting differs by category dependent on levels of interest, involvement and risk. We judge customer services from a bank very differently to those from a grocery supermarket or a computer store.

The three main factors are Trust, Treatment and Delivery.

Trust = trust in the brand X level of recommendation X transparency / honesty.

Treatment = friendly service X efficiency X speed

Delivery = quality of product X value for money and / or cost

Such a measurement could become an annual barometer through which companies monitor their competitive performance against both their sector and against the general feelings of the country.

The area is probably more important now than ever. Poor treatment of employees and customers has never been acceptable but was taken less seriously in the past as it could be kept quiet. Nowadays, reputations can be destroyed in the blink of an eye through social media and elsewhere. It can take a lot longer to repair the damage.

Take the example of David Carroll. This is an old story now but still relevant. If you are not familiar with it, David, a musician, was travelling between USA cities on a United Airlines flight when, through the plane window, he saw baggage handlers throw his prized guitar into the luggage hold thus breaking it. He had been told that the guitar couldn't travel with him in the cabin.

He complained to the airline and was ignored. He complained again, and again. He wrote. He e-mailed. He telephoned countless times still with no satisfactory response.

After nine frustrating months (clearly David is a patient man) he wrote a song called 'United Breaks Guitars' and made a video. It was uploaded and attracted millions of hits in a very short period of time. I awoke to see the item on BBC Breakfast News in London by which time it had been shown in several countries. A girlfriend emailed me having seen it in Australia.

The result? 10% ($180 million) was wiped off the United Airlines share price. One customer, one complaint, badly handled, massive consequences, big lesson for all.

Everyone makes mistakes. Big companies included. But some use the ostrich approach like United while others turn a bad experience into a good one.

I called American Express recently as I was annoyed. A significant amount of interest had been added to my bill when I was only very slightly late in paying.

If I was gagging for an argument I was sorely disappointed. Within seconds I was told that the charge would be removed as I am a 'valued' customer and always pay on time. I was obviously pleased but not only because the decision was in my favour, I was impressed mainly because Amex has empowered its staff to be able to take immediate decisions such as this. This is positive customer feedback and now I am telling you.

Contrast my American Express experience with those from Lloyds Bank and Asda. What do they have in common? Very little apart from both having ATM machines and green logos but both are companies in which I will never set foot again because of the appalling way I was treated by staff.

I don't need to go into details but the problem in both cases, unlike Amex, was that employees were not empowered to make decisions. When I said I would take my business elsewhere (Lloyds) and never come back (Asda), it was clear that neither company cared a jot. Lloyds call centre told me leaving was my prerogative. I was further annoyed as I had been with Lloyds for a very long time and considered myself to be a good customer but no-one even contacted me to ask why I had left. Maybe I just wasn't as important as I thought! Maybe they were glad to see the back of me. Why should they care? They are big successful companies and I am but one tiny, insignificant customer. Well they should care - I had bad customer experiences and now I am telling you. We had no social media in those days.

> **Brands are defined by what consumers say to each other about them, not what a brand says to consumers.**
>
> David Jones
> 'Who Dares Wins'

I am puzzled as to why companies don't recognise the value of empowering staff. Employees, the company and its customers will benefit. Whether the company is big or small, has many employees or few, operate in retail, manufacturing or even in a media agency, all categories of business should encourage staff to act as ambassadors for their business. They should be considered as a key communications channel and included in the communications planning process.

But Lloyds and Asda pale into insignificance compared with the treatment I received from W. J King, a Kent Kia car dealer where I had my car serviced regularly. I was put into a potentially life-threatening situation due to negligent servicing. I wrote a very strong letter of complaint and received this reply:

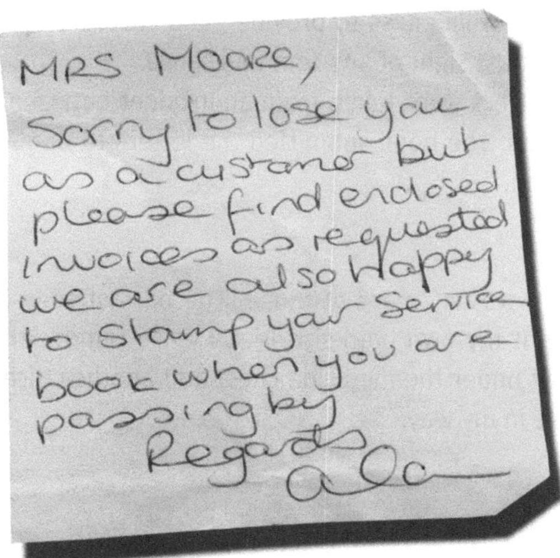
MRS Moore,
Sorry to lose you
as a customer but
please find enclosed
invoices as requested
we are also Happy
to stamp your service
book when you are
passing by
Regards

Can you believe it? It's a post-it note. You couldn't make it up. Needless to say, my business has been lost forever.

Clearly hell hath no fury like a woman scorned by customer services but I wonder if any of these companies considered my lifetime value to their business.

Let's put it this way. Sainsbury, Waitrose, the Clydesdale Bank and little Denis Motors have benefited greatly from bad treatment from their competitors. It's pathetic to bear a grudge for such a long time but putting it in print felt so good.

I don't think that delivering good customer service is difficult neither need it be expensive. It just needs a bit of thought from the perspective of the customer.

Andy Setchell, to whom I dedicated this book, and I used to carry out an exercise that we called the 'Mr and Mrs Miggins' test. Mr and Mrs Miggins are fictional characters who we imagined were reacting to every research question, every communication, every presentation, every strategic decision and tactic. They were just ordinary people with real lives unlike us city advertising folk living in our bubbles. If we thought Mr and Mrs Miggins wouldn't understand or wouldn't like what we were doing then we had to re-think. I think many companies could do well to have such a barometer.

On a lighter note, here is an old but amusing little tale from a hotel where the staff demonstrated a willingness to provide good customer service but, in the process, completely lost sight of any common sense.

The following letters were taken from an incident between a London hotel and one of its guests. The hotel submitted the letters to the Sunday Times for their humour column.

Dear Maid

Please do not leave any more of those little bars of soap in my bathroom since I have brought my own bath-size Dial. Please remove the six unopened bars from the shelf under the medicine chest and another three in the shower soap dish. They are in my way.

Thank you

S. Berman

Dear Room 635

I am not your regular maid. She will be back tomorrow. I took the 3 hotel soaps out of the shower soap dishes you requested. The 6 bars on your shelf I took out of your way and put on top of your Kleenex dispenser in case you should change your mind. This leaves only the 3 bars I left today. My instruction from the management is to leave 3 soaps daily. I hope this is satisfactory.

Kathy

Relief Maid

Dear Maid

I hope you are my regular maid. Apparently, Kathy did not tell you about my note concerning the little bars of soap. When I got back to my room this evening I found you had added 3 little Camays to the shelf under my medicine cabinet. I am going to be here in the hotel for two weeks and have brought my own bath size Dial so I won't need those 6 little bars that are on the shelf. They are in my way when shaving, brushing teeth etc. Please remove them.

S. Berman

Dear Mr Berman

My day off was last Wednesday so the relief maid left 3 hotel soaps which we are instructed by the management. I took the 6 soaps which were in your way on the shelf and put then in the soap dish where your Dial was. I put the Dial in the medicine cabinet for your convenience. I didn't remove the 3 complimentary soaps which are always placed inside the medicine cabinet for all new check-ins and which you did not object to when you checked in. Please let me know if I can be of further assistance.

Your regular maid
Dotty

Dear Mr Berman

The assistant manager Mr Kensedder, informed me this morning that you called him last evening and said you were unhappy with your maid service. I have assigned a new girl to your room. I hope you will accept my apologies for any past inconvenience. If you have any further complaints please contact me so I can give my personal attention. Call extension 1108 between 8am and 5pm. Thank you.

Elaine Carmen
Housekeeper

Dear Miss Carmen

It is impossible to contact you by phone since I leave the hotel for business at 7.45 and don't get back before 5.30 or 6pm. That's the reason I asked Mr Kensedder if he could do anything about those little bars of soap. The new maid you assigned to me must have thought I was a new check in since she left another 3 bars on the bathroom shelf. In just 5 days I have accumulated 24 little bars of soap. Why are you doing this to me?

S. Berman

Dear Mr Berman

Your maid Kathy has been instructed to stop delivering soap to your room and remove the extra soaps. If I can be of further assistance please call extension 1108 between 8am and 5pm. Thank you

Elaine Carmen
Housekeeper

Dear Mr Kensedder

My bath-size Dial is missing. Every bar of soap was taken from my room including my own bath-size Dial. I came in late last night and had to call the bellhop to bring me 4 little Cashmere Bouquets

S. Berman

Dear Mr Berman

I have informed our housekeeper Elaine Carmen of your soap problem. I cannot understand why there was no soap in your room since our maids are instructed to leave 3 bars of soap each time they service a room. The situation will be rectified immediately. Please accept my apologies for the inconvenience.

Martin L Kensedder

Assistant Manager

Dear Mrs Carmen

Who the hell left 54 little bars of Camay in my room? I came in last night and found 54 little bars of soap. I do not want 54 little bars of soap. All I want is my bath-size Dial. Please give me back my bath-size Dial.

S. Berman

Dear Mr Berman

You complained of too much soap in your room so I had them removed. Then you complained to Mr Kensedder that all your soap was missing so I personally returned them. The 24 Camays that had been taken and the 3 Camays that you are supposed to receive daily. I don't know anything about the 4 Cashmere Bouquets. Obviously your maid Kathy did not know I had returned your soaps so she also brought you 24 Camays plus the 3 daily Camays. I don't know where you got the idea that this hotel does bath-size Dial. I was able to locate some bath-size ivory which I left in your room.

Elaine Carmen

Housekeeper

Dear Mrs Carmen

Just a short note to bring you up to date on my latest soap inventory. As of today I possess:

- On the shelf under the medicine cabinet - 18 Camay in 4 stacks of 4 and 1 stack of 2
- On the Kleenex dispenser - 11 Camay in 2 stacks of 4 and 1 stack of 3.
- On the bedroom dresser - 1 stack of 3 Cashmere Bouquet, 1 stack of 4 hotel-size Ivory and 8 Camay in 2 stacks of 4.
- Inside the medicine cabinet - 14 Camay in 3 stacks of 4 and 1 stack of 2.
- In the shower soap dish - 6 Camay very moist.
- On the northeast corner of tub - 1 Cashmere Bouquet slightly used.
- On the northwest corner of tub - 6 Camays in 2 stacks of 3.
- Please ask Kathy when she services my room to make sure the stacks are neatly piled and dusted. Also please advise her that the stacks of more than 4 have a tendency to tip. May I suggest that my bedroom window sill is not in use and would make an excellent spot for future soap deliveries. One more item, I have purchased another bar of bath-size Dial which I am keeping in the hotel vault to avoid further misunderstandings.

S. Berman

Only in England!!

Moving back to customer service, I think that the tech companies should give us a better deal. They have swept us along on an exciting digital journey but, on the way, have stripped away our rights to privacy and protection.

At this stage it is tempting to rant about the behaviour of the tech giants. They provide some wonderful products and services many of which we would find difficult to live without. Where we object is when we feel our data may be misused and abused.

There are lots of paradoxes here. On the one hand, we don't want to be tracked everywhere we go but, on the other, Google maps are wonderful. We don't want companies knowing everything about us but love the customer service provided by Amazon. And so on.

But here's the thing. When purchasing from a shop, I choose my item, I pay my money and it is mine. If I buy the same item on-line, I cannot do so without agreeing to an endless number of terms and conditions. Why? Why can't I just buy it like I would in a shop? It's simply a different delivery method.

The GDPR regulations don't go far enough in fact they have started to work against us. I lost a cinema membership card recently but the cinema couldn't access my information on their system to issue a replacement because of the rules of GDPR. I am now being protected from my own data. Has the world gone mad?

I tried to buy some theatre tickets from an on-line ticket agency recently and decided to take a look at their terms and conditions - you know, the ones we all just agree to without checking.

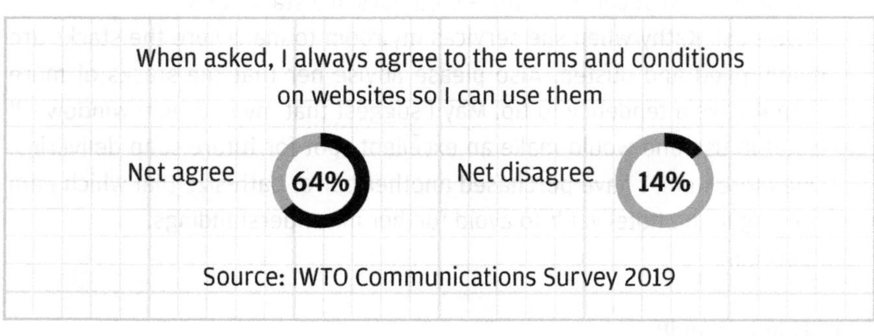

When asked, I always agree to the terms and conditions on websites so I can use them
Net agree
64%
Net disagree
14%
Source: IWTO Communications Survey 2019

They went on for what seemed like an eternity. Here are just a few of the T's and C's that I came across:

- 'If you choose not to share your personal information with us, or refuse certain contact permissions, we may not be able to provide you with some services that you have asked for'.

My response: Contact permissions? You are seriously prepared to withhold tickets and refuse my money because I won't allow you to flog my personal details?

- 'We may also receive information about you from independent organisations that we have worked with. You should check their privacy policy when you provide your information to them to understand fully how they will process and safeguard your data'.

My response: Who are these 'independent organisations' that you have worked with? How do I I know who to check?

- 'We will collect personal information that may include, but not be limited to, name, contact details, information about your gender, payment information, CCTV images'.

My response: Information about my gender? CCTV images? WHAT? WHY?

- 'In the course of providing our goods and services we may collect information that could reveal your religious beliefs or your health'

My response: be reminded that I am simply buying theatre tickets. But here they may have a serious point. People without sound religious belief or a healthy disposition should not be allowed into theatres. Keep 'em out. That's what I say.

- 'We share your data with other companies in the group as an essential part of being able to provide our services to you'.

My response: Sorry? Why is this essential? And how do we know who is in the group?'

- ' We use your personal data to train our staff'.

My response: those training sessions must be a gas. Sign me up immediately.

In the end I abandoned the screen, purchased the tickets over the 'phone and didn't have to agree to anything.

Examples like this are very annoying as online transactions can be the best - easy, fast and efficient, what could be better? There must be fantastic opportunities for companies to provide services that simply replicate the in-store experience without collecting or doing anything with our data.

If I had a choice when shopping online, I would choose a company that didn't collect personal data about me rather than one that did
Net agree
55%
Net disagree
8%
Source: IWTO Communications Survey 2019

I think it's time to fight back. We are not just data points, we are real people.

Perhaps we should create our own Customer Terms and Conditions, a 'customer charter' to which companies would have to agree before we agree to buy from them. Our conditions would be straightforward and only one page rather than the endless, deliberately bamboozling Ts and Cs that no-one can be bothered to read. It would go something like:

- I agree to purchase (the product) providing that you agree to the following terms and conditions:
- No further use will be made of my name, address or any other personal details apart from information relating to the purchase and delivery of the product I have bought from you.
- No marketing information will be sent to me unless I have expressly agreed.
- None of my personal details will be passed to any third parties irrespective of whether or not they are an associated business.
- In agreement with my terms and conditions, you agree to delete all data you hold on me apart from details relating to the purchase and delivery of this purchase.
- You also agree to instruct any associate companies or other parties to whom you have previously passed on or sold my data to delete all information held on me.
- If you fail to agree to my terms and conditions then I withdraw my order and you agree to provide a full refund.

A couple of weeks after writing the above section, I came across a speech by Brian O'Kelly who was speaking before the Senate Judiciary Committee.

O'Kelly has had fifteen years of building advertising technology in partnership with the world's largest digital publishers and marketers. He helped to build Right Media that was bought by Yahoo and was co-founder of AppNexus that was acquired by AT&T.

The crux of his speech was that "the lack of competition in the internet sector is harming consumers and preventing innovation". In addition, he said, "I believe that consumers need rights to protect their personal data". Here is a section from his speech:

"We need a data bill of rights that establishes some first principles for what consumers should expect from companies that have access to their data. Some basic principles that we might start with:

- I want to know any time that someone collects data about me.
- I want to know where that data resides and that it is properly protected from cyber-security attacks.
- I want to give explicit permission before that data is shared with another service, even if that service happens to have the same corporate parent.
- I want the ability to correct or remove my data.
- I want the ability to take all of my data with me, in a usable form, and transfer it to another company or service."

OK I know - my customer charter is probably silly, unworkable and too simplistic But Brian O'Kelly is an expert in such matters and appears to thinking along similar lines. It feels as if we have been bludgeoned into the digital commercial world without a full understanding of the implications. Perhaps it is time to fight back.

I will if you will.

Some

final thoughts

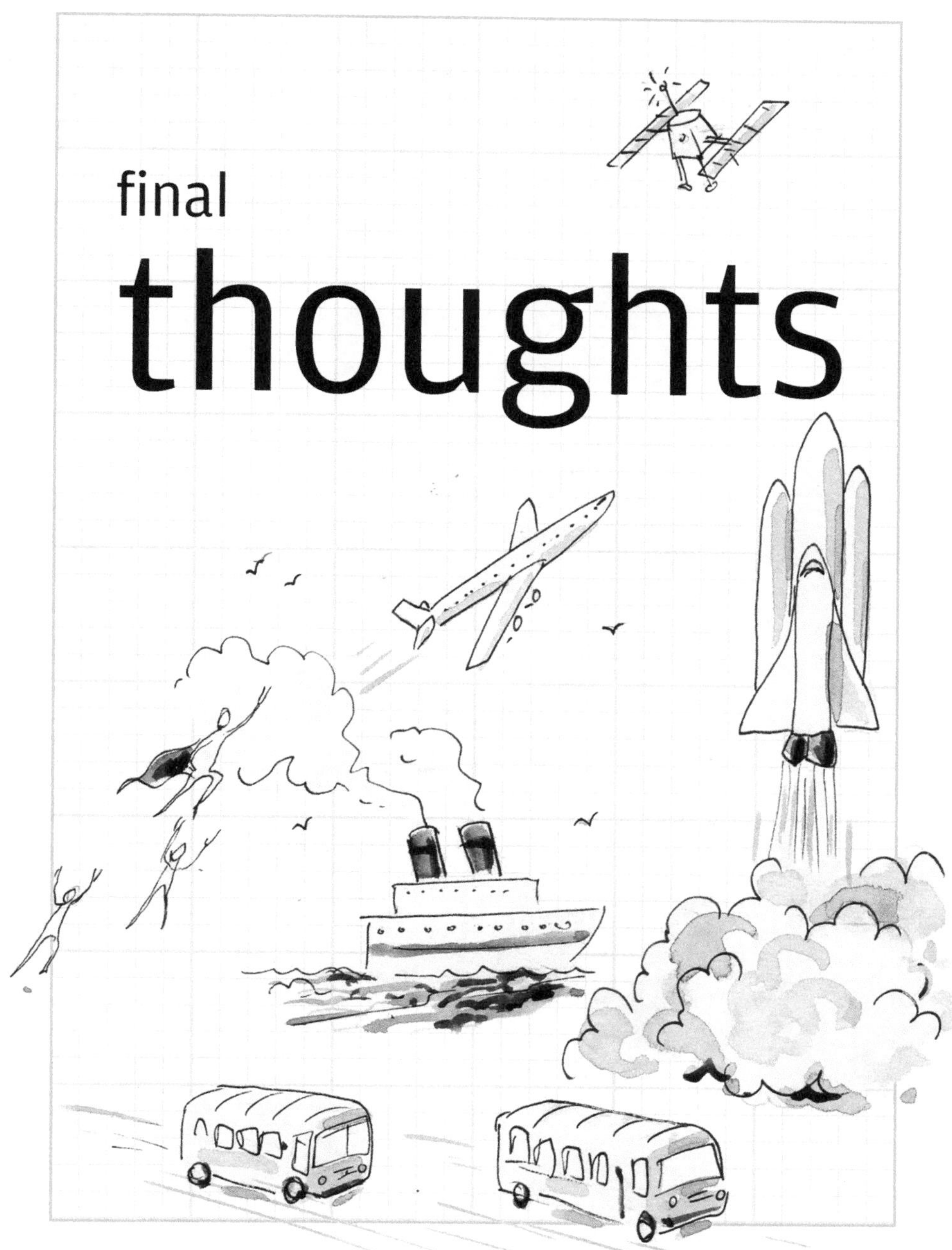

“When I sit down to write a book, I do not say to myself, ‘I am going to produce a work of art.’ I write it because there is some lie that I want to expose, some facts to which I want to draw attention and my initial concern is to get a hearing”

George Orwell

Some final thoughts

Well, there is no doubt that 'In With The Old, In With The New' is not a work of art but there were facts to which I wanted to draw attention and the book has provided a hearing.

I have enjoyed the ranting and only hope that they have offered some food for thought. If, at the end of it, you feel that there may be a benefit of returning to basics and using common sense when planning communications with the public - or if it has re-enforced such views - then this may have been worthwhile.

I have tried to summarise my main points below

- Everyone involved in communicating with the public needs to swallow a big, healthy dose of reality and common sense. Do your friends and family understand what you do? Do they understand the jargon that you use? Would your language pass the Mr and Mrs Miggins test? If not then take a big step back and re-invent your language in everyday speak.

- The media and advertising businesses are running the risk of becoming boring when they used to be exciting and fun. It's not about holding endless parties but people should be encouraged to talk with one another, share ideas and exchange experiences. How much of the day is spent away from a screen? How much time is spent just thinking? When I was at Mindshare, our team held a weekly Friday afternoon meeting that we called 'Tea and Cakes'. Apart from eating delicious, naughty, squidgy treats the objective was to 'dump the week'. We shared our work and helped one another with problems and challenges. It was such a small initiative but it encouraged team spirit, knowledge sharing and involvement. Meetings were great fun and a huge success.

- We need to recognise that people in ad land do not reflect the population at large. Every staff member working on a brand should have a KPI to meet with, and gather insights from, its target audiences. They should be asking questions of people at the point of purchase, go outside the major cities to talk to real people living real lives. Everyone should be allowed time away from the office to visit retailers, study purchasing behaviour, talk with target groups about their brand choices, discover why they choose your brand, discover why they choose competitive brands and then return with fresh insights - not from data or existing research but from real life observations and conversations. Valuable banks of information and insights will build quickly. Staff will gain valuable experience. They with thank you. Your clients will love you.
- Everyone involved in any aspect of advertising should be trained on all aspects of the business and its disciplines. Introduce a Certificate of Excellence to prove core and advanced competencies. Publicise it. Make it an industry badge of honour. This is something to which employees can aspire and be proud and it will stand them in good stead for moving up the career ladder. Your clients will feel that they have the crème de la crème of talent working on their business. It's a win, win, win situation.
- Organise events / conferences for clients, the media and industry professionals. Invite leaders to share experiences from various aspects of the business both from inside and outside the communications arena. Cover areas such as psychological, social / cultural trends or a specific demographic. Trawl through the academic world to find potential speakers. Topics like 'the truth about women today' (or men, or millennials, or children, or social media, or television viewing, or technology trends and so on) will always attract a good crowd, give you lots of PR and heaps of credit from clients.
- The hype surrounding the digital revolution was unprecedented. Digital media offer exciting, powerful, effective communications opportunities but the most successful aspects are not really advertising in the context that we have defined it up until now. They also don't hold the answers to every brand challenge. The fit with the brand strategy must come first. Les Binet and Peter Field have provided excellent guidelines on the most effective balance between brand advertising and activation and between digital and other channels. Every

media professional should have studied their work and be well versed on the findings.

- For every media placement, attention should be paid to why people are there, how much time pressure they might be under and whether the message will fit the context. Ask common sense questions about data generated solutions. Make sure that what is going into databases is sufficiently balanced to provide confidence in what is coming out.
- There is a serious need to go back to basics. If you talk with customers about their brand experiences they will most likely talk of practical attributes such as how the brand tastes, how it looks, whether it works, whether they like it or not. They will rarely talk to you about a brand making them feel wanted, human, loved, moved, empowered, released or any other emotion that we try and force people to describe. The exception to this may be businesses such as leisure and catering but even then people often talk more about taste and comfort rather than about feeling 'moved' by their experience. In his book 'The Ten Principles Behind Great Customer Experiences', Matt Watkinson suggests that each company should have a CXO (Chief Experience Officer) member of its C Suite. He is right.
- The most valuable people in any organisation are the people who work in it. How often do CEOs and CMOs meet with people on the shop floor and in customer services? How often do they spend time in the call centre listening first hand to everyday challenges? I am not talking about listening to boardroom presentations from heads of department or reading the latest customer satisfaction survey. I mean getting down and dirty and mucking in. Public facing employees are the most valuable people in the company to tell you how you are really doing. Involve them, they will feel valued and try harder. Every employee represents the brand - what are they saying about you?

Above all, keep it simple and remember the words of George Bernard Shaw:

“ **Common sense is instinct. Enough of it is genius** .

Acknowledgements

I have been knocked out by the generosity and kindness of many people whose help has been invaluable in illustrating the issues that I wanted to address.

I would like to offer my sincere thanks to the following:

Marcel Baker : production and design

Robert Dance : data analyses

Doreen Dignan : management of quantitative survey and chart production.

Daniele Fiandaca : permission to reproduce the essay by Sam Ball and Dave Bedwood from Digital Advertising: Past, Present and Future.

Karen Fraser MBE: data from Credos. The Advertising Association.

Matt Hill: data Thinkbox analyses and data.

Belinda Beeftink, Kay Heenan, Janet Hull and Rebecca Watson from The Institute of Practitioners in Advertising (IPA) for providing access to Touchpoints data and to charts and text from 'Effectiveness in Context' by Les Binet and Peter Field.

Robert Laurence and James Powell, Kantar Media for TGI data.

'The Master and His Emissary' text was reproduced from an episode of 'The Hidden Brain presented by Shankar Vedantam and broadcast by NPR.

Mindshare: for the opportunity to wander around the world conducting wide-ranging research and to have a ball while doing it.

Jo Peters: qualitative research management.

Nick Sami for editing and proof reading.

The industry professionals who kindly gave their precious time and effort to record their views:

Alison Ashworth: OMD

Professor Patrick Barwise: The London Business School

Jenny Biggam: the7stars

Andy Brown: Kantar Media

Nick Emery: Mindshare

Andrew Green: IPSOS

William Higham: The Next Big Thing

Bob Hoffman: The Ad Contrarian

Brian Jacobs: Independent consultant

Katherine Page: Freelance consultant

Rory Sutherland: Ogilvy

Book References

Life After Television. The Coming Transformation of Media and American Life. George Gilder.

Being Digital. Nicholas Negroponte

Beyond the Familiar: Long Term Growth through Customer Focus and Innovation. Patrick Barwise & Sean Meehan.

Creative Blindness and how to cure it. Dave Trott

Digital Advertising: Past, Present and Future. A collection of essays edited by Daniele Fiandaca and Patrick Burgoyne

Everybody Lies. Seth Stephens-Davidowitz.

Marketers Are From Mars, Consumers Are From New Jersey. Bob Hoffman.

The Master and his Emissary. Iain McGilchrist

Simply Better: Winning and Keeping Customers by Delivering What Matters. Patrick Barwise & Sean Meehan.

Social Media Marketing. Liana “Li” Evans.

Television and its audience. Patrick Barwise & Andrew Ehrenberg.

The ten principles behind great customer experiences. Matt Watkinson

The Undercover Economist Strikes Back: Tim Harford.

Freakonomics: Professor Steven D. Levitt

L - #0058 - 200819 - C0 - 210/148/13 - PB - DID2595434